DEEPENING DISCIPLESHIP

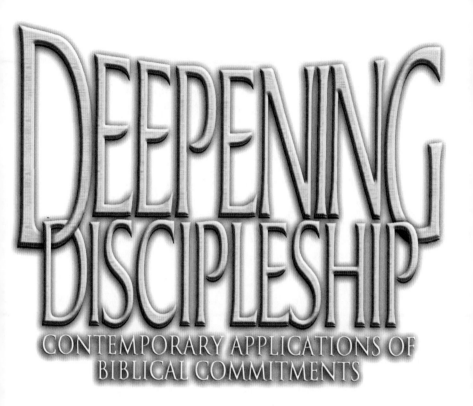

DEEPENING DISCIPLESHIP

CONTEMPORARY APPLICATIONS OF BIBLICAL COMMITMENTS

Oliver McMahan

Foreword by R. Lamar Vest

Pathway
PRESS
Cleveland, Tennessee

Book Editor:	Wanda Griffith
Editorial Assistant:	Tammy Hatfield
Copy Editors:	Cresta Shawver
	Oreeda Burnette
Cover Design:	Wayne Slocumb
Inside Layout:	Gwendolyn Westfield

Library of Congress Catalog Card Number: 00-101814
ISBN: 0-87148-274-6
Copyright © 2000 by Pathway Press
Cleveland, Tennessee 37311
All Rights Reserved
Printed in the United States of America

DEDICATION

To my family:

My wife, *Martha*,
my daughter, *Holly*,
my son, *Jonathan*,
my daughter-in-law, *Heather*,
and my two granddaughters,
Haley Marie and *Sarah Beth*.

Table of Contents

Foreword

Success and failure in life may be judged in different ways, but Scripturally based integrity focuses on inward priorities. The ability to integrate discipleship values with our outward responses is critical to our Christian walk.

In *Deepening Discipleship*, Dr. Oliver McMahan describes various components of integrity formation that revolve around love—loving God and loving our neighbors as ourselves (Matthew 22:37-40). Written as a Biblical commentary for contemporary application of the Practical Commitments of the Church of God, Dr. McMahan discusses six areas that shape personal integrity and aid the flow of discipleship values:

- Spirituality and godly character

- Emotions

- Thinking

- Behavior

- Relationships

- Surroundings

Researching the original minutes of the Church of God, the author documents the concerns of the early leaders of our denomination and organizes them into three sections. The first two sections frame the Practical Commitments according to two great commandments, that is, love the Lord with all your heart and love your neighbor as yourself. The third section organizes the last third of the Practical Commitments around the witness of the believer's life to the world. The historical background of these commitments identifies a rich source for understanding the deepening flow of discipleship.

Ultimately, a Christian's personal integrity will reveal the character of Christ. The flow of the presence of Christ in the believer does not diminish the reality of Christ. On the contrary, Christ is glorified through His disciples.

God's Word outlines this walk: "With all lowliness and meekness, with longsuffering, forbearing one another in love; endeavoring to keep the unity of the Spirit in the bond of peace" (Ephesians 4:2, 3). The author shows how the life of the church is directly correlated to the integrity of individual believers.

This book will challenge you to establish and deepen your discipleship values; and, through it, you will receive practical instruction and specific directions for carrying out Christ's commands.

—Dr. R. Lamar Vest
General Executive Committee
Church of God
Cleveland, Tennessee

Acknowledgments

Grateful acknowledgment goes to the excellent staff of Pathway Press, who made this book possible—*Dan Boling*, general director of publications; *Bill George*, editor-in-chief; *Wanda Griffith*, book editor; *Tammy Hatfield*, editorial assistant; *Pat Bradbury*, director of marketing; *Wayne Slocumb*, graphic designer; *Homer Rhea*, former editor-in-chief; and many others.

Introduction

Discipleship is a growth process that begins when we accept Christ. From its source—the Word of God—the flow of discipleship begins, constantly moving, continually growing, rounding bends, making adjustments . . . but ever expanding.

The flow of discipleship described in Ezekiel 47, began with the presence of God in the holy temple. As it moves out from His presence and proceeds down the mountain of God, the waters expand. Other streams and rivers join the flow until a river is formed. As Ezekiel was brought further downstream, God's message to him was "Follow the flow, move further downstream and I will show you depths in Me that produce life." Everywhere the waters of Ezekiel flowed, there was life.

Today the waters of discipleship flow over rocks, desert places and many other obstacles. No matter what the circumstances, the waters keep flowing throughout the course of life. Contemporary challenges and every-day struggles cannot impede the growth of true discipleship as long as we follow the standards set by our Savior and keep moving as He directs.

This book is written as a Biblical commentary for contemporary application of the Practical Commitments of the Church of God. These commitments were designed to give direction and Biblical values to Christians as they moved downstream in their Christian lives. Like the measurement of the waters of Ezekiel 47, discipleship values mark the depth and growth of the believer's walk of faith.

In this book, the Practical Commitments are organized into three sections. The first two sections frame the first two-thirds of the Practical Commitments according to two great commandments, that is, love the Lord with all your heart and love your neighbor as yourself. The third section organizes the last third of the Practical Commitments around the witness of the believer's life to the world.

Introductory and summary chapters emphasize the role of the Holy Spirit in the discipleship process. The scripture references supporting the Practical Commitments are exegeted and integrated into contemporary living. Even the historical background and roots of these commitments are identified as a rich source for understanding the flow of discipleship.

The overall message of *Contemporary Applications of Biblical Commitments* is that discipleship values are relevant in the 21st century. From God's mighty power flows the waters of Christian living. Understanding and applying these values promote growth in the life of the believer.

I encourage you to step into the waters of discipleship. Follow the flow. Move downstream into the deeper waters of Spirit-filled living.

CHAPTER ONE

BUILDING INTEGRITY

Faith and victorious living are outgrowths of the presence of personal integrity. If personal integrity has been properly emphasized, godly living will follow. On the other hand, if personal integrity is absent, faith and victory will be difficult, if not impossible.

Success and failure may be judged in different ways, but Scripturally based integrity focuses on our inward priorities. Personal integrity is the ability to integrate these discipleship values with our outward responses in the development of faith.

Dynamics of Personal Integrity Formation

Personal integrity has two parts in its essential definition. Personal defines the individual nature of the process. *Integrity* comes from the Latin *integrare* ("integer" or "integrate") and means to maintain the congruency of various parts into a whole or unity. Therefore, personal integrity is the skill of maintaining the congruency of the parts of our existence. The lack of personal integrity is the inability to bring these various aspects of life into agreement.

Scripture addresses two basic parts of our existence— the inward spirit and soul, and the outward public life. The agreement of these forms the center of personal integrity. In order to have personal integrity, we must live publicly what we profess privately.

Old Testament roots. The word *integrity* in Scripture finds its root in the Old Testament word *tom*, which means "to be complete." *Completeness* indicates the genuineness of someone or something. Regarding things, the integrity of an object is determined by whether it really is what it claims to be. For example, is a metal really gold or is it imitation? Regarding persons, integrity deals with whether or not an individual's heart is really what the person claims to be. The essential agreement between the internal claims of the heart and external actions reveal the formation of discipleship values and integrity.

The importance of personal integrity was the theme of Isaiah 1. After declaring the burden of Israel's sin in the first 11 verses, the Lord declared the travesty of their worship in verses 12-14. Each part of their worship was analyzed and found wanting. Finally, the most intimate and personal acts of devotion were captured in verse 15 with the phrase, "When ye spread forth your hands." Their hands were "full of blood"—the most convicting of all the assessments.

The fact that the Israelites' personal devotion was corrupt made everything else they did corrupt. They had become abusive to one another. Even though their worship was very elaborate, their failure in personal devotion made the rest of their actions unacceptable to God. Personal formation (the values we truly live by) is the foundation of our life before God. No matter what we accomplish in life, our integrity and values will be the criteria by which God sees us.

Jesus' definition. Jesus defined personal integrity when He was confronted by the Pharisees in Luke 11 and 12. He told them that it did no good to clean the outside and neglect the inside (11:39). Further, the inward part would be revealed eventually (12:2, 3). He declared that not only should the two agree, but also that the inward part must be developed first in the fear of the Lord (12:4-7).

Godly fear indicates a two-fold emphasis in the formation of personal integrity. The first emphasis is that priority be given to the development of discipleship values and integrity. The second emphasis is devotion to God. The words most often used for "fear" in the phrase, "the fear of the Lord," were *yare* (Old Testament) and *phobeo* (New Testament). These words indicated that the believer should be "overwhelmed" by God, rather than by anything else. The fear of the Lord must place commitment to God first and foremost. This constitutes the first principle in the formation of integrity.

The word *Jesus* used in Luke 11 and 12 to describe the opposite of godly fear was *hypocrisy*. This describes someone who tries to develop integrity by placing first priority on external formation, rather than the inward formation. *Hypocrisy* means "someone wearing a mask," indicating an individual who was one thing on the outside but something else on the inside. This incongruence is always the outcome when the development of personal integrity is either corrupted, or the greater priority has been placed on externals and material living.

The power of devotion and the formation of integrity are much greater than the external forces of worldly pressure. Internal commitment to Christ should be a first priority, and the application of integrity in public life should never be compromised because of external pressure.

In another passage, Jesus stressed the importance of integrity when He called the disciples to single-hearted devotion (see Matthew 22:37-40). He admonished them that despite the hypocrisy of the Pharisees and pressure to compromise, they were to remain faithful (Matthew 23).

Impact on All Areas of Life

There must be congruence between four areas.

- Individual

- Marital/familial

- Professional

- Corporate

The agreement between the inward condition of the heart and the actions displayed in these four areas form the essence of integrity and Christian values. Two tendencies generally occur when integrity is compromised.

Hypocrisy develops when the external does not match the actual condition of the heart (see Luke 11 and 12). With continued corruption of the heart, external actions will eventually be corrupted as well. On the other hand, personal integrity and the presence of discipleship values will be revealed in the believer's actions.

The boundaries of personal integrity and value formation. The process of developing personal integrity and values is defined by the parameters of God's Word. Believers are not free to live according to their own whims and choosing. God's Word becomes the guide for the Christian.

The six areas that shape personal integrity are inner spirituality and godly character, emotions, thinking, behavior, relationships and surroundings. The development of these areas helps to strengthen skills in the formation of personal integrity and aid the flow of discipleship values.

1. *Spirituality and godly character.* Some of the elements necessary in this area are repentance, spirituality, worship, conscience and godly fear. *Repentance* is the essential catalyst that makes godly character possible. *Spirituality* affirms this is an inward, spiritual task. *Worship* is essential because character is formed as the soul and spirit exalt God. *Conscience* identifies the primary level of intuitive functioning that determines the formation of character and integrity. The importance of *godly fear* has already been discussed.

Inward spirituality must be maintained as the first priority in the development of personal integrity. The effectiveness and proper development of the other areas described depends on the maturity and Spirit of God within the person. This can only be realized through the power and presence of the Holy Spirit working within that person.

2. *Emotions: affections, cares and intimacy.* Emotional development depends on spiritual development. If formation of inward spirituality and godly character are not the central priority of a believer's life, then desire and emotions avert the heart away from personal integrity.

Elements that influence the development of emotional integrity include affections, cares and intimacy. *Affections* indicate emotions that are the basic reflection of the spirit and priorities. *Cares* are the reflection of emotional responses to external pressures and competing priorities. Finally, *intimacy* is the personal nature of emotions that are felt privately and yet reveal the priorities of character and integrity. *Emotions* will guide the development of integrity or drive the impulses of hypocrisy.

3. *Thinking: concentration, will and perception.* *Thinking* is the ability of an individual to focus the godly intents of the heart on effective application. Proper development of thinking depends on spiritual maturity. If spiritual development is not a priority in a person's life, it can be the passage by which external priorities are distorted and given erroneous perception.

Areas which make up thinking include concentration, will and perception. *Concentration* of one's resources, whether internal or external, is done through the mind. The *will* sets these resources in a certain direction, with or without integrity. *Perception* is how information is processed. It can be done in such a way that godly integrity is enhanced or a compromise of values is justified.

4. *Behavior: discipleship and habits.* Inward spirituality and godly character are the foundation for godly behavior. What is in the heart will eventually be revealed in behavior.

Two factors that make up behavior formation are discipleship and habits. *Discipleship* reveals that behavior is set by learning patterns established through godly character. We act as disciples of some principle or person. Behavior is not merely generic. *Habits* indicate behaviors that become routine and automatic. Having acted in response to the priorities and conditions of the heart, habits become a reflection of who we really are, revealing our level of integrity.

5. *Relationships: love and faithfulness.* Although integrity begins in the heart, it is also exemplified in our relationship with others. Godly relationships between

individuals are possible because of the foundational relationship between an individual and God.

Two significant components that make up relationships are love and faithfulness. *Love* is not a condition of the heart—it is a barometer of relationships. *Faithfulness* is denoted in the longevity and strength of those relationships. Integrity formation takes place in the context of relationships, never in isolation.

6. *Surroundings: avoidance and stress.* The final component of the formation of discipleship values is *surroundings.* As with the previous areas, inner spirituality and godly character form the foundation for a person's ability to deal with his or her surroundings effectively. Areas that define the level and kind of relationship we have to our surroundings include avoidance and stress. Our integrity is formed as we filter, (i.e. *avoid*) those areas that distract us from our walk with God. The failure to properly filter our lives for Christian effectiveness results in *stress* and ineffectiveness. An overload of stress indicates the testing or breaking down of integrity. The effective utilization of stress indicates that the congruency between personal and godly character is being maintained, despite the demands of the world around us.

The Paradigm of Philippians 4:8-11

Philippians 4:8-11 is an excellent example of the apostle Paul communicating the components that comprise the development of personal integrity.

> Finally, brethren, [components] whatsoever things are true, whatsoever things are honest, whatsoever things are just, whatsoever things are pure, whatsoever things are lovely, whatsoever things are of good report; if there be any virtue [inner spirituality], and if there be any

praise, [components] think on these things. Those things, which ye have both learned, and received, and heard, and seen in me, do: [development in faith and practice] and the God of peace shall be with you. But I rejoiced in the Lord greatly, that now at the last your care of me hath flourished again; [components] wherein ye were also careful, but ye lacked opportunity. Not that I speak in respect of want: for I have learned, in whatsoever state I am, therewith to be content.

The words Paul uses to emphasize spirituality and godly character include *virtue, true, praise* and *honest. Virtue* is single-hearted devotion to God that creates excellence of character (Greek, *arete*). *True* is the maintenance of congruence between the heart and the public formation of actions and relationships (Greek, *apelegmos*). *Praise* is the response for commendable public actions (Greek, *eapinos*). *Honest* was a well-known Greek concept, *semnos*, which expressed the gravity of honest character.

The words Paul uses to emphasize emotional development include *lovely* and *content. Lovely* (Greek, *prosphiles*) and *content* (Greek, *autarkees*) are emotional states expressing the godliness of inner character.

The words that emphasized thinking were *just, think* and *learned. Just* (Greek, *dikaios*), *think* (Greek, *logizomai*) and *learned* (Greek, *manthano*) are words expressing the criteria and thinking process by which personal integrity was maintained.

The words that emphasize behavior are *pure* and *do. Pure* (Greek, *hagnos*) and *do* (Greek, *prasso*) express the criteria and actions of one's integrity expressed in behavior.

The words emphasizing relationships are *good report* and *in me. Good report* (Greek, *eupheema*) and *in me* appeal to the basis of personal relationships in the formation of personal integrity.

The words emphasizing surroundings are *state, heard* and *seen*. They relate to the awareness and response of an individual's surroundings and relationships in the formation of personal integrity.

Moving From Inside to Outside

Integrity formation has been described in this chapter as a process of maintaining congruence between the inward life of the believer and the outward life. Various components of that process have been reviewed. The components and process occur in three different aspects, all of which revolve around love. The first aspect is the process as it occurs in the believer—*loving God with all your heart.* This causes the believer to be changed and challenged. Discipleship values affect the believer's own life, bringing growth and maturity in Christ.

The second aspect is *loving others as yourself.* Christ taught a gospel that is directed toward others in that the values of Christians impact others, not only the believer.

The *world* is the third aspect of the formation of the believer's discipleship values. Ultimately, the values of the believer convey God's love to all the world.

The process of these three aspects can be illustrated with the following diagram:

These three aspects of love and the formation of discipleship values will be discussed in the rest of the book as the three primary divisions for a Christian's discipleship values.

Church of God Historical Review

There are a number of examples of discipleship values from the early history of the Church of God. The Church of God began in 1886 as a fellowship and Bible study group. By 1906 a number of churches had begun and the church had an identity. As a body of believers meeting at various locations, the churches would gather together into a central meeting once a year. The first central meeting, called the General Assembly, was in 1906.

The minutes of those early General Assemblies indicate that much of the discussion centered around discipleship values. This review captures various topics of the first General Assembly meetings.

In the 1907 General Assembly "sects, doctrines, opinions and divisions" were discussed (*General Assembly Minutes,* 1907, p. 20).

After reading a part of 1 Timothy 4, A.J. Tomlinson said, "There are so many sects, doctrines, opinions and divisions that it is of vast importance for us to know the truth as contained in the Scriptures." After speaking at some length on the different "doctrines of devils" in vogue today, the speaker took up the subjects on the program and briefly outlined the important features one by one, advising the speakers to stand out boldly for their convictions, having themselves so clothed with love that no one could be hurt and always ready to yield to plain Scriptural teaching, even though it might cross some former views. The plain Bible teaching, rightly divided, to settle all controverted points.

This section indicates that the connection between heartfelt love and right doctrine was vital. The audience was admonished to be clothed with love; attitude was just as important as content.

There was also concern that discipleship values be lived out. Again, when discussing the importance of right doctrine, we find another emphasis on living what you believed. This kind of commitment as it related to heresy and behavior continued in the early years of the Church of God. The following section of the 1919 General Assembly Minutes titled "Heresy" indicates this:

> While this vile enemy [heresy] is running rampant in the land, doing his deadly work, we have had little trouble with it in the Church. Making a mistake in dividing Scripture is not heresy, when it is merely because of a lack of knowledge. Unintentional teaching that is contrary to sound doctrine is not necessarily heresy. But we very much desire that all of our teachers hold steadfastly to the Apostles' doctrine, and teach that which they know the Church stands for rather than venture into something that will be detrimental to the cause we love. Heresy is an opinion or doctrine at variance with fundamental truths commonly received by the Church as orthodox, especially if leading to division. It is the division we must prevent. Individuals may get up some heretical notions and have to be excluded, but there must be no divisions (*General Assembly Minutes,* 1919, p. 16).

This description of heresy highlights both belief and behavior. Belief as a body of knowledge is emphasized in the middle section of the discourse, referring to the apostles' doctrine and orthodox teaching. Behavior is referred to in the beginning and ending sections. Heresy is viewed as a matter of personal intent and divisive behavior. False doctrine is not defined merely by its content. Personal intention and sinful striving against the body are also identified with heresy.

The inner life of the disciple was important. In the early General Assembly meetings the leaders clarified at

25

various times that discipleship values were about priorities of the heart, not just behavior. An example is a statement from the general overseer that the emphasis move from externals to condition of the heart.

> Some have gotten into erroneous ideas because they do not see the weightier things and the reason of this is for a lack of knowledge. It might be well to speak of coffee occasionally in private conversation. . . . We should be careful about saying harsh, rasping things about it that would wound the feelings of our brothers and sisters. Pork may not be good for some people and we might all be better off if we did not use it, but if one wants to eat it another does there should be no fault-finding with each other about it. 'The kingdom of God is not meat and drink; but righteousness, and peace, and joy in the Holy Ghost.' . . . It is good for people to appear neat in dress, and in many places you would have no influence with the people for good if you did not wear a collar and perhaps a tie. People sometimes become proud in going slouchy as others in vain dress (*General Assembly Minutes*, 1913).

CHAPTER TWO

THE PERSONAL LIFE OF THE BELIEVER

As believers love God, they find that His love provides the substance and power for other values to develop. Discipleship values must be personally applied. If believers are not personally motivated to live a life of integrity, then all values are questioned.

Three discipleship values are formed within the context of loving God: *spiritual example, moral purity* and *personal integrity*. Spiritual example is shown by the depth of a personal relationship with God. Moral purity is possible because of the work of God within. Integrity is a result of an individual's walk with God.

There are three primary aspects of our love for God:

- Standing in a relationship of peace before God because of God's justification and love for the believer;

- Walking consistently as a follower of God as the character of that love; and

- Being reconciled to God through the work of Christ as a result of that love.

Peace With God (Romans 5:1, 6-10)

"Therefore being justified by faith, we have peace with God through our Lord Jesus Christ: By whom also we have access by faith into this grace wherein we stand, and rejoice in hope of the glory of God" (Romans 5:1, 2). Positive relationships are built on the foundation of a proper relationship with God. This relationship has been described in many ways throughout Scripture. One description is "having peace with God." The peace the believer has with God comes from a relationship of justification and love from God. The justification relationship is described in the first part of verse 1. The word *justified* comes from the Greek *dikaioo* and means "to declare to be righteous or in the right." No one can have peace with God without being justified before Him.

Dikaioo comes from a root concept, *dika*, which means "to be after a certain kind." The word represents "conformity to a standard or order." As a result, the word *dikaioo* raises the question of standard. Someone may be considered "justified," but the real question is, "By what standard?" Justification is only as good as the standard to which the individual is "conformed" or justified.

The believer's justification is obtained by satisfaction of God's standard. Christ conformed to the standard of the Father on our behalf. Therefore, through Christ the believer has been conformed to God's standard. Peace with God is the result of justification. The word *peace* comes from the Greek *eireeneeh,* which emphasizes "quietness and rest." The New Testament authors understood it in the context of the Old Testament meaning of

28

the Hebrew *shalom*. It means not only "peace" but also "complete or whole." It does not necessarily mean the absence of conflict. Despite a person's condition, there can be a sense of completeness in God.

Paul used *eirenee* (or *peace)* in Romans to depict the believer's relationship with God. This peace comes only from God (1:7) and is available to all believers (2:10). This "way of peace" is not known by sinners (3:17). It is the result of spiritual mindedness (8:6)—a vital part of the gospel (10:15). This peace is essential in the kingdom of God (14:17), and it is part of Paul's admonishment to the believer (14:19; 15:13, 33). Finally, it is the God of peace who will defeat Satan (16:20).

Paul's use of *eirenee* in Romans 5:1 assures the believer of peace with God. The substance and content of this peace is real—whole and complete. However, even more important than the content is the relationship upon which the peace is grounded. This is not peace alone, but peace with God.

Peace through Christ's work of love. "But God commendeth his love toward us, in that, while we were yet sinners, Christ died for us" (v. 8). Paul illustrates how dependent we are on Christ for peace. Christ made the provision for this peace when no one else could. We were "sinners" (v. 8). This word means that we "missed the mark." No one is qualified to receive peace with God, much less make it possible for others.

Nevertheless, because of Christ's work, the Father "commendeth" His love toward the believer. *Commendeth* comes from a Greek word that means "to place with" or "demonstrate." It emphasizes bringing something into reality. Peace with God was made real only because Christ died for the sinner.

Peace from the wrath of God. "Much more then, being now justified by his blood, we shall be saved from wrath through him. For if, when we were enemies, we were reconciled to God by the death of his Son, much more, being reconciled, we shall be saved by his life"(vv. 9, 10). Here Paul describes the condition opposite to peace with God—the wrath of God. The believer is saved from God's wrath as a result of Christ's work. The word, *saved*, is presented in the Greek text as a definite event. In other words, salvation from wrath is not merely a hope, but a reality.

The word *wrath* refers to the judgment of God. Those who are not justified through Christ will receive this His judgment in return for transgression and disobedience.

In verse 10 Paul clarifies the condition of those who will receive the wrath and judgment of the Lord. Sin is not a private matter. It effects our relationship with God. Anyone who refuses the work of God's precious Son remains an enemy of God.

Peace with God is a precious privilege of the saints . . . a dear treasure purchased by Christ's precious blood. The wrath of God is no longer the destiny of a person. Rather, the individual who believes, immediately enjoys the benefits of peace, wholeness and union with God.

Living as God's Children (Ephesians 5:1-7)

"Be ye therefore followers of God as dear children" (v. 1). Besides peace with God, another important description of the believer's relationship with God is following Him as obedient children. In similar fashion, the believer is to be a trusting and submissive follower of the Lord.

Paul begins Ephesians 5 by appealing for the readers to be followers of God. The word *followers* comes from the Greek *mimatas*. The English word *mimic* is derived from this word, which means to "imitate." This is especially true in a moral sense. Every occurrence of the word in the New Testament is in the context of moral living (*The Vocabulary of the Greek New Testament* by Moulton and Milligan).

The word *as* indicates that what is to follow is the "characteristic quality" (*A Greek English Lexicon of the New Testament,* by Bauer) of what it means to be a "follower of God." This is a primary trait of a follower of God—someone who as a "dear child" lovingly follows and obeys his or her parent.

God's children walk in love. "And walk in love as Christ also hath loved us, and hath given himself for us an offering and a sacrifice to God for a sweetsmelling savour"(v. 2). Paul calls the Christian's manner of life a "walk of love." *Walk* refers to someone's "conduct of life." Love is the boundary that defines that walk. The standard by which the believer's love is to be measured is Christ's own love. The word *as* sets this standard. Paul highlights Christ giving Himself for the lost. He did so "for us as an offering." This was an act of worship. Following Christ is an act of love to the Father that benefits others. The relationship of the believer to others is the result of a right relationship with God.

God's children forsake uncleanness. "But fornication, and all uncleanness, or covetousness, let it not be once named among you, as becometh saints; Neither filthiness, nor foolish talking, nor jesting, which are not convenient: but rather giving of thanks" (vv. 3, 4). The believer's relationship with God is marked by specific commitments. At times "loving" and "being a child before the heavenly Father" are seen as abstracts. They are not specifically defined. However, Paul specifically defines what it means to have a loving relationship before God.

This definition in Ephesians includes six prohibitions and one affirmation. The first three prohibitions emphasize personal selfishness. The process is *fornication, uncleanness* and *covetousness. Covetousness* summarizes these and means "to be greedy." All refer to practices that fulfill personal lustfulness.

The last half of verse 3 places these prohibitions in the context of faithfulness to God. Avoiding them is not just an act of self-improvement—it is a matter of consistent faithfulness to God.

The second group of prohibitions emphasizes relationships with others. *Filthiness* refers to actions that are shameful and obscene. *Foolish talking* and *jesting* refer to speech that harms others.

As with the first group, the second group of prohibitions reflects on our relationship with God. Doing them is not *convenient*. This word means "to be fitting." They are not part of the Christian life because they represent a haughty spirit rather than a thankful one to God.

God's children do not partake with sinners: "For this ye know, that no whoremonger, nor unclean person, nor covetous man, who is an idolater, hath any inheritance in the kingdom of Christ and of God. Let no man deceive you with vain words: for because of these things cometh the wrath of God upon the children of disobedience. Be not ye therefore partakers with them" (vv. 5-7).

Paul emphasized the impact our relationship with others has on our relationship with God. In verses 3 and 4 he addresses how the believer's relationship with God should affect relationship with others. He reverses the emphasis in verses 5 through 7.

We are influenced by others; no one lives entirely alone. The people we associate with help shape our lives. We become a reflection of them, and they become a reflection of us. If the believer is consistently influenced by unbelievers, there will be a mutual effect. The degree and nature of this mutual effect is the topic of verses 5 through 7.

Different kinds of unbelievers are listed in verse 5. These include *whoremongers,* the *unclean,* the *covetous man* and the *idolater. Whoremonger* comes from the Greek word *pornos.* It is the same word from which the English word *pornography* is derived and refers to someone who has succumbed to sexual immorality. *Unclean person* refers to someone who does not live a morally pure life. *Covetous* means to be "greedy" and self-centered.

Idolater summarizes the previous items listed. They all are a result of a life without God, a life given over to worshiping something or someone else. Without a believing relationship with God, a person is subject to these practices. This is the backdrop of Paul's warning to the believers.

Verse 6 stresses God's judgment on those who are not committed to Him. Many are deceived by thinking that God does not hold them accountable for their disobedience. Greed and selfishness are evil, but the greatest tragedy is when God sees believers become corrupted by disobedience.

Partakers means "to possess the same," and stresses the kind of relationship where one person influences another. It refers to matters of the heart more than practice. Paul was warning believers not to allow the sentiments and commitments of the world to influence them.

Reconciled to God, the Result of Loving God (Colossians 1:19-23)

Reconciled by Christ. "For it pleased the Father that in him should all fullness dwell; And, having made

peace through the blood of his cross, by him to reconcile all things unto himself; by him, I say, whether they
be things in earth, or things in heaven" (vv. 19, 20).

Though a great gulf has separated us from God, provision has been made for our reconciliation. It is God's
will for us to have a relationship with Him. This will is
captured in the word *please*. Our relationship with God
is birthed in His good pleasure. Even before we accept
the Lord, God is already expectantly waiting for us.

All fullness refers to the completeness within Christ to
accomplish reconciliation. The fullness of deity within
Christ makes His work eternal. The humanity of the
Incarnation made His work a reality that could be
received by us. This work was complete—thoroughly
adequate to bring mankind to the Father.

In verse 20 Paul emphasizes that Christ has reconciled
all things to Himself. The word Paul uses here in the
Greek for *reconcile* is not a common word. Some scholars believe it may have been a special expression Paul
only used in verse 20 and in Ephesians 2:16 to emphasize exchanging hostility for friendship.

The distinction of this verse is that Christ reconciles
"all things." The concept of reconciliation is usually in
reference to God and the believer. However, the phrase
here refers to all of creation and all the powers of heav-
en and earth. Christ's blood on the cross affirmed that all
creation is under Him. No doubt the false teachers in
Colossae had been teaching that some things were not
subject to Christ. However, the work of Christ includes
the reconciliation of all things to Himself and His
dominion.

Condition before reconciliation. "And you, that were
sometime alienated and enemies in your mind by wicked
works, yet now hath he reconciled." Verse 21 describes

the condition of the believer prior to reconciliation. The believer was "alienated" and an "enemy" of God. *Alienated* is derived from a Greek word meaning, "to be shut out from fellowship and intimacy." The word was used in some ancient literature to describe evil estrangement and separation between a married couple. *Enemy* can be translated, "hostile ones," because it denotes a conscious antagonism.

Prior to faith in Christ, the believer was alien and hostile to God in his "mind" because of his "wicked works" (v. 21). *Mind* comes from a Greek word that refers to the heart, emotions and spiritual nature. In this verse it includes all of these aspects as well as mentality.

In contrast to the wicked condition in which a person is separated from God, Christ reconciles the believer to Himself. *Reconciled* emphasizes the transformation of hostility into a close, vital relationship. This was accomplished through the sacrifice of Christ.

Reconciled condition of the believer. "In the body of his flesh through death, to present you holy and unblameable and unreproveable in his sight" (v. 22). The purpose of Christ's reconciliation was to present the believer "holy and unblameable and unreproveable in his sight." There are two types of *presenting* emphasized in this verse. The first is *sacrificial* and the second is *legal*.

The sacrificial presentation is based on the words *holy* and *unblameable*. These words were used in the Old Testament to describe the requirements for sacrificing animals. In Christ, the Father examines believers and finds them acceptable for a life of sacrifice and service to Him.

The legal idea of *presenting* is based on the term, "unreproveable," a legal term that referred to a person who had no accuser. No legal claims could then be made against that person. In Christ, believers are brought before God, the Judge, and no charges of sin are brought against them. The Christian's relationship with God is established in freedom.

Continuing in reconciliation. "If ye continue in the faith grounded and settled, and be not moved away from the hope of the gospel, which ye have heard, and which was preached to every creature which is under heaven; whereof I Paul am made a minister" (Colossians 1:23). The believer must continue in a reconciled relationship with God. It is a permanent relationship so long as the believer remains faithful. The possibility to walk away from this relationship does exist. This is why Paul exhorted them to continue in faithfulness.

Grounded and *settled* describes the way to continue in faith. These words are typically used in reference to the construction of a building. *Grounded* refers to a properly laid foundation. *Settled* refers to the firmness of a structure.

The believer's relationship with God is one than cannot be moved as long as the believer holds on to Christ as the foundation. This foundation cannot be broken, but we can remove ourselves from that foundation. Other foundations and relationships can be sought. At that point, no matter how firm the foundation of Christ, it's benefits are no longer experienced.

Application of Principles

The dynamics of loving God with all your heart need to be applied in Christian living. The following suggestions will facilitate this application.

1. *Maintain a strong personal devotional life as the foundation for living.* Skills in personal devotion such as

prayer, Bible reading, personal worship before the Lord and others form the groundwork from which other skills in living can be developed.

2. *Use personal devotions as a resource for developing other areas of life.* For example, the kind of love God imparts to you in your personal walk with Him can direct you in how you are to love others.

3. *Recognize that your relationship with others is a reflection of your personal relationship with God.* This does not mean that your relationships with others is perfect. However, the way you respond to these relationships reflects the kind of relationship you have with the Lord.

Developing Discipleship Values

Loving God and the resulting peace and lifestyle that develops from this relationship creates important discipleship values. As mentioned earlier in this chapter, three discipleship values are developed out of the believer's love for God. The first of these, spiritual example, is the subject of chapter 3.

ELEMENTS OF A SPIRIT-FILLED WALK

Spiritual example as a discipleship value for the believer can be defined by the following statement. The definition is presented as a commitment statement for believers.

Spiritual Example

We will demonstrate our commitment to Christ through our practice of the spiritual disciplines; we will demonstrate our commitment to the body of Christ through our loyalty to God and commitment to His church; and we will demonstrate our commitment to the work of Christ through our being good stewards.

There are certain practices that illustrate what it means to be a spiritual example. These practices can be grouped under the following topics:

- Spiritual disciplines

- Loyalty to God and commitment to the church

- Being good stewards

There are key scriptures that give instruction to the believer about how to be a spiritual example. Therefore, God's Word is the foundation of discipleship values for the believer. Scripture shines through the Christian, glorifying Christ before shining upon the believer, highlighting any particular accomplishment or ability.

Practice of Spiritual Disciplines

Spiritual disciplines involve such practices as prayer, praise, worship, confession, fasting, meditation, and study. Through prayer we express our trust in Jehovah God, the giver of all good things, and acknowledge our dependence on Him for our needs and for the needs of others (Matthew 6:5-15; Luke 11:1-13; James 5:13-18).

Through both private and public worship we bless God, have communion with Him, and are provided daily with spiritual enrichment and growth in grace. Through periods of fasting we draw close to God, meditate on the passion of Christ, and discipline ourselves to submit to the control of the Holy Spirit in all areas of our life (Matthew 6:16-18; 9:14-17; Acts 14:23).

Through confession of our sins to God we are assured of divine forgiveness (1 John 1:92:2).

The sharing of our confession with other believers provides the opportunity to request prayer and to bear one another's burdens (Galatians 6:2; James 5:16).

Through meditation on and study of the Word of God we enhance our own spiritual growth and prepare ourselves to help guide and instruct others in Scriptural truths (Joshua 1:8; Psalm 1:2; 2 Timothy 2:15, 23-26).

Personal spirituality is the starting place for spiritual example. Several disciplines, as noted in the statement of the last paragraph, mark our spiritual condition. These include prayer, fasting, confession of sins, bearing one another's burdens and meditating on the Word.

Prayer. Jesus admonished the disciples to pray sincerely to the heavenly Father (Matthew 6:5-15; Luke 11:1-13). They were to pray honoring God and not men as the hypocrites did. He gave them a model prayer to follow that honored God and sought His forgiveness as they forgave others (Matthew 6:12; Luke 11:2-4). Luke said to ask persistently in prayer (11:5-13). James emphasized the power of the prayer of the righteous, especially when done in Christian love for those who are sick (James 5:13-18).

Fasting. Matthew recorded that the hypocrites fasted with a sad countenance to draw attention to themselves (Matthew 6:16-18). On the contrary, people who were fasting should anoint their head and wash their face so that they do not appear to be fasting. The presence of Christ should be at the center of fasting (9:14-17). Jesus explained to the disciples of John that fasting was a time to rekindle the memory of the presence of Christ, similar to the presence of a bridegroom and new wine. In Acts 14:23, fasting is part of the commissioning process of believers and elders in the church.

Confession of sins. In 1 John 1:9 and 2:2, John says that if the believer had sinned, he had an opportunity to receive forgiveness from the Father. He was not saying that a Christian had to sin or was bound to sin. Rather, he was saying that if sin did occur, forgiveness was provided.

Bearing one another's burdens. Paul admonished the Galatians that bearing one another's burdens was at the heart of the commands and teachings of Christ (Galatians 6:2). Christ expects believers to love one another, expressing that love by sincere care for each other. Bearing burdens and fulfilling the command to love are mutual acts. James declared to his readers that healing and righteousness were available through care for one another (James 5:16). These were displays of the power resident in bearing each other's burdens.

Meditating on the Word. Certain passages list the benefits of meditating on God's Word. Those who meditated on God's Word will be prosperous (Joshua 1:8). They will not be subject to the same perils and pitfalls of those who fail to do so (Psalm 1:2). They are to pursue the Word with a deep fervency. In 2 Timothy 2:15 the word *study* refers to an intense, constant pursuit of God's Word, as opposed to mere intellectual exercises.

Loyalty to God and Commitment to the Church

The life of Christian discipleship calls for the fulfillment of our duties to the body of Christ. We are to unite regularly with other members of the church for the purpose of magnifying and praising God and hearing His Word (Matthew 18:20; John 4:23; Acts 2:42, 46, 47; 12:24; Hebrews 10:25).

Sunday is the Christian day of worship. As the Lord's Day, it commemorates the resurrection of Christ from the dead (Matthew 28:1) and should be employed for worship, fellowship, Christian service, teaching, evangelism, and proclamation (Acts 20:7; Romans 14:5, 6; 1 Corinthians 16:2; Colossians 2:16, 17).

We are to provide for the financial needs of the church by the giving of tithes *(Malachi 3:10; Matthew 23:23) and offerings (1 Corinthians 16:2; 2 Corinthians 8:1-24; 9:1-15). It is our duty to respect and submit to those whom the Lord Jesus has placed over us in the church (1 Thessalonians 5:12,13; Hebrews 13:7, 17).*

Our exercise of authority must be as a spiritual example, rather than as a lord over God's flock (Matthew 20:25-28; 1 Peter 5:1-3). Furthermore, our submission must be a manifestation of the spiritual grace of humility (Ephesians 5:21; 1 Peter 5:5, 6).

Finally, we are to avoid affiliation with oath-bound societies. Such societies may appear to have spiritual character, but by being oath-bound and secretive, they contradict Christian spirituality (John 18:20; 2 Corinthians 6:14-18). Christians must not belong to any body or society that requires or practices an allegiance that supersedes or excludes their fellowship in Christ (Matthew 12:47-49; John 17:21-23).

The outgrowth of a committed personal life before the Lord is a commitment to others in the household of faith. Spirituality is not complete simply by going through acts of personal commitment. Loyalty to the community of believers is required as well. Several priorities are necessary for genuine commitment to other believers. These include uniting regularly, observing the Sabbath, giving of tithe and offerings, submitting to each other in the Lord with an attitude of humility and avoiding oath-bound societies controlled by secrecy.

Uniting regularly. This was a strong practice of the early church because they knew that Christ had given extra assurance about His presence in the midst of His saints as they gather together (Matthew 18:20). Gathering together is to be highlighted with worship in spirit and in

43

truth (John 4:23). The gathering of the saints is to be marked by fellowship, sharing, witnessing, worshiping and doing the work of God (Acts 2:42, 46, 47). The gathering of the saints, especially in the face of persecution, is rewarded by an increase in the witness of the Word of the Lord (Acts 12:24). Finally, the command to gather together and exhort one another is especially true as the Lord's coming approaches (Hebrews 10:25). Gathering together helps preserve and protect the saints as they endure until the day of His appearing.

Sunday. The women who cared for Jesus' body were careful to observe the Sabbath, even though it stood in the middle of the time that they were to prepare His body for full burial (Matthew 28:1). The Sabbath is to be observed because of the Lord and not mere human requirements (Romans 14:5, 6). It is also to be a time of giving offerings to God because He has prospered the believer (1 Corinthians 16:2).

The observance of the Sabbath is to be centered on Christ and His commandments (Colossians 2:16, 17)—a sacred time that reflects the enduring faithfulness of a believer in response to the abiding love of God unto us.

Tithe and offerings. Tithing is not only a command, but it is also a challenge from the Lord to trust Him for blessings (Malachi 3:10). Tithing does not produce spirituality, but it is a reflection of someone who has learned to place proper priority on spiritual matters (Matthew 23:23).

As mentioned under the heading of *Sunday*, believers are to give to God because of His abundant gifts to them (1 Corinthians 16:2). Paul dealt extensively with the subject of translating care for other believers into giving in offerings and monetary support (2 Corinthians 8:1-24). He also gave a major exhortation regarding faithfulness to God in giving because God had been so abundant in His provision to him personally (2 Corinthians 9:1-15).

Submit. Submission is a major portion of the Christian life. This is to be done with love, giving high regard to those over us in the Lord and the work they have extended to us (1 Thessalonians 5:12, 13). Submission was seen by Paul as an act of peace (1 Thessalonians 5:13). Those over us in the Lord are to be held accountable for their manner of life and faithfulness to the Lord. This is the most influential part of their witness (Hebrews 13:7).

Authority. Those who serve in positions over others in the Lord are to mark their authority with the characteristics of service and ministry (Matthew 20:25-28). They are to be an example to others in Christian faith and godly character (1 Peter 5:1-3).

Humility. Submission and humility are reflections of a strong spiritual life (Ephesians 5:21). They grow out of the control of the Spirit and a worshipful lifestyle (Ephesians 5:18-21). Humility is to be the foundation for godly living between husband and wife (Ephesians 5:21—6:4). God will actively bless those who maintain a humble spirit, but He will resist those who refuse to humble themselves before God and others (1 Peter 5:5, 6).

Oath-bound societies. Secrecy was a serious topic with Christ. His ministry and life before others was not marked by a cloud of secrecy (John 18:20). Paul strongly admonished against developing intense or binding relationships on the level of communion and unity with those who are not believers (2 Corinthians 6:14-18). Rather, the Lord should set priorities for the believer. The Lord emphasized the control and will of the heavenly Father rather than the control of individuals (Matthew 12:47-49). The Christian's life and affiliations should reflect the priority of unity with Christ and the heavenly Father. Affiliations, especially those that are binding and controlling relationships with groups, are contrary to the Lord's command to live in unity with Him (John 17:21-23).

Being Good Stewards

In the Scriptures, the virtues of thrift and simplicity are honored, but the vices of waste and ostentation are solemnly prohibited (Isaiah 55:2; Matthew 6:19-23). The living of a godly and sober life requires the wise and frugal use of our temporal blessings, including time, talent and money. As good stewards we are to make the most of our time, whether for recreation or for work (Ephesians 5:16; Colossians 4:5). The idle use of leisure time degrades (2 Thessalonians 3:6-13; 1 Timothy 5:13), but the edifying use of it brings inner renewal. All our work and play should honor the name of God (1 Corinthians 10:31). As good stewards we must use fully our spiritual gifts (Romans 12:3-8; 1 Corinthians 12:1-11, 27-31; Ephesians 4:11-16; 1 Peter 4:9-11) and natural talents (Matthew 25:14-30) for the glory of God. As good stewards we must recognize that the wise use of money is an essential part of the Christian's economy of life. God has committed temporal blessings to our trust (Matthew 7:11; James 1:17).

The concept of stewardship emphasizes God's resources. The steward is not the owner of the things he manages—he is merely the caretaker of property and privileges owned by another person. Christians must use what is available to them as stewards, realizing that God, the One who has provided, owns everything. Priorities that emphasize godly stewardship include a godly perspective on simplicity and waste, wise use of time, godliness in work and play, use of spiritual gifts, godly direction for the use of natural talents and the Biblical use of money.

Simplicity and waste. Those who have their hearts set on God are rewarded with contentment. Isaiah asked about this reward. The admonition he gave in Isaiah 55:2

46

highlighted satisfaction as the result of diligently seeking the Lord. The Lord himself warned against the practice of depending on the resources of this world. Worldly resources fade away and are subject to theft and erosion. Material wealth should not be the foundation for a person's life (Matthew 6:19-21).

Time. The apostle Paul seriously addressed the wise and godly use of a person's time. In Ephesians 5:16 he spoke of the necessity of "redeeming" or "taking opportunities" with our time. This was in comparison to the works of evil. As evil takes time from individuals, the believer is to correspondingly take time back to use it for God's kingdom. In Colossians 4:5 Paul emphasizes the need for wisdom to be a witness before others of God's work in the life of the believer. Responsible use of time and labor is a witness before God and helps others in the body of Christ (2 Thessalonians 3:6-13). Furthermore, idleness, the foolish and wasteful use of time, is a reflection of the spiritual condition of a person (1 Timothy 5:13).

Work and play. How we use our leisure time is a reflection of our commitment to the Lord. It manifests our personal preferences and priorities. This does not mean that recreation should be a serious time. Rather, the focus of our leisure activity should be a witness of God's work in our lives (1 Corinthians 10:31). The same principle applies to all of our activity—including work.

Spiritual gifts. Passages in Romans 12:3-8; 1 Corinthians 12:1-11, 27-31; Ephesians 4:11-16; and 1 Peter 4:9-11 list a number of spiritual gifts. They are not the mere stimulation or exercise of natural abilities, innate within a person. They represent what God has given to establish His kingdom. With the exercise of these gifts, the believer should be more aware of their origin than just their manifestation. The Gift-giver is still more important than the gift.

Natural talents. The parable of the talents in Matthew 25:14-30 identifies important characteristics for stewardship. The talents came from the master, not the servants. The talents were given according to the wisdom and perception of the master. The stewards were expected to carry out the effective use of their talents. The primary criterion for their effectiveness was obedience. To be obedient, goodness and faithfulness were required. The servant with one talent did not use what was given him because he did not think the master was honest. His relationship with the master was not right. This was the basis of his lack of effectiveness.

Money. Money should not be viewed as a burden, but as a blessing that God desires to bestow upon His children. However, this blessing requires a relationship where the child of God is dependent on and obedient to the heavenly Father (Matthew 7:11). The possessions and blessings of God, including money, are gifts from God. They are not the product of man's labors (James 1:17).

Applying the Scriptural dynamics of becoming a spiritual example is not automatic. Developing discipleship values on the basis of spiritual disciplines takes hard, consistent work. Specifically, how can the believer live out discipleship values that translate into regular disciplines of being a spiritual example? The following are suggestions that will assist in that transformation.

Practice of Spiritual Disciplines

The priority of personal spirituality. Before believers can help others, they must have received care from the

Lord themselves. Believers cannot give direction to others until they have received direction from the Lord. There can be no greater message to others than the personal testimony of God working within an individual's own life.

To help individuals grow in faith and practice, believers must first experience their own personal spiritual walk and example before they can become a witness to others in the church and the world. Whether the spiritual condition of the believer is fervent or lukewarm, others will be affected either positively or negatively. The more effective and responsible position is to use personal spirituality as a foundation for reaching out to others.

Specifying personal disciplines. A number of personal disciplines will be specified in this section. These included prayer, fasting, confession of sin, bearing burdens and meditation on the Word of God.

Believers must not just talk about personal spirituality in general—they must specify the components of spirituality. Vague commentaries about spirituality is not fair to others. Believers lives and values give direction as to exactly how a person can mature spiritually. The specific disciplines listed in this section are a starting place. There are other personal spiritual disciplines such as memorization of Scripture, intercessory prayer, and personal times of praise in the Spirit that should be emphasized.

Loyalty to God and Commitment to the Church

Interpreting the church as a spiritual commitment. The church is not an institutional commitment. Many individuals believe that the church is merely an organization, composed of systems, hierarchies and facilities.

The commission of Scripture regarding the church was not about an organization of individuals. The church and the commitment of its laity are not merely a group of individuals with finely tuned structures and allegiances.

In the local church, each believer's commitment of being faithful to one another is part of being faithful to the Lord. Christians become a part of the body of Christ, not by their own choices, but they are made part of the body of believers known as the church by the act of the Lord. Their commitment of faith is not only to the Lord, but it is also a spiritual initiation into the group. As a consequence, the relationship a person has to the church is always a spiritual one. It goes beyond a mere mental commitment or a gathering of people who have a common purpose. The call to believe in the Lord is inseparable from the call to gather in His name.

Effective Christian values must couch the disciplines of mutual commitment listed in this section as faith commitments that are carried out in obedience to the Lord.

Church leaders, such as pastors, can build on faith commitments to the church; however, they cannot build for eternity on organizational commitments. The latter will crumble because it is only as strong as the organization. However, an emphasis on commitments to Lord and the church will yield lasting results and bring the church and its individual members in line with the call of Christ.

As each member commits to the church, Christ truly builds the church by channeling His actions into the life of the church. When individuals see their commitment as only to other persons and not to Christ, they block the flow of God's power into the life of the church. It is their work and not the work of Christ that is done. Church then becomes merely the collection of the work of men and women committed to one another rather than the work of Christ expressed through their unified commitment to Christ.

Specifying commitments to the church. If commitment to the body of believers is left to vague generalities, believers will wander. Effective Christian values specify the nature of the believer's commitment to the church. Attendance in church, participation in activities, tithing, submission and all the other areas mentioned in this section express how believers translate theirs faith in Christ to commitment to the body.

The organization of the local church should be seen as a method of maximizing the use of God's resources. The organization of a meeting or the scheduling of certain events are not merely decisions to do something that has always been done before, they are commitments of believers to effectively use God's resources.

Without genuine stewardship, people in the church will come to believe that what they accomplish is the result of their own labor. As a result, pride and self-centeredness can easily creep in. Effective churches focus on the process in which the church specifies how it will use God's resources (personally and corporately) in acts of faithful stewardship.

Church of God Historical Review

This section will show ways in which the Church of God has historically believed in being a spiritual example. The concept is not a new one in the church. Each of the major ideas of personal spiritual disciplines, being loyal to God and committed to the church and being good stewards appears in the history of the church as recorded in the early minutes of the General Assembly of the Church of God.

Prayer meetings discussed by brother Alex Hamby and others. It is, therefore, the sense of this Assembly that we recommend, advise and urge that the local churches hold a prayer-meeting at least once a week. We recommend further, that some one in every Church, who may feel led by the Holy Spirit, or selected by the church, take the oversight thereof and see that such prayer-meeting is held regularly in proper order (p. 14, 1906 General Assembly Ledger).

This resolution about prayer meetings shows an early, strong emphasis upon the priority of prayer in the church. It received the designation of an actual service. Prayer was to be a personal discipline and a highlight of the church. The believers were to gather not only for worship services but also times specifically given over to the ministry of prayer. Prayer was an important spiritual discipline to them.

This emphasis was demonstrated in the proceedings of the General Assembly. The early assembly minutes note frequent times of prayer. At the end of a critical session, prayer would be offered up to the Lord. In the midst of a difficult decision, prayer would break out. The occurrence in the assembly and recording of these events shows that prayer was an important priority of theirs.

In the General Overseer's remarks in the 1917 General Assembly, a major appeal was made to "Deeper Spirituality." In his address, A.J. Tomlinson stated the following:

Special attention should be given at all times to the deepening of the spirituality of the members. There should be a sense of spiritual freedom at all times in the services. When we are made free through Christ, then it we must retain that freedom. Remember the exhortation of our dear Brother Paul who said, "Stand fast therefore in the liberty wherewith Christ hath made us free, and be not entangled again with the yoke of bondage." Our people should be encouraged to yield to the Spirit, and even to stir up the gift that is in them. Preaching is necessary, but if all of our services are given to preaching only, the spiritual fire would go out. There must be testimonies, talking in tongues, interpretations, signs, wonders, dancing and whatever else the blessed Spirit of God dictates. Our people must be in the Holy Ghost. This freedom must not be taken away from them. A part of almost every service should be given to these free exercises in the Spirit. Then the preaching will be enjoyed better—it will do more good. The letter alone will kill, but the Spirit gives life. These outpourings are as juice or flavoring to the Word. They are necessary for the best interests of all the children of God. It has been said that there is more liberty, and rejoicing, set out among the Church of God people than any people on earth. We must retain our reputation, and not become dead and formal. I have thought we could make the most noise, and then suddenly change to the most intense quietness, above any people on earth. The Lord tells us to make a joyful noise unto Him, and He also says for us to be still and know that He is God. Thus we are changed and wafted about by the blessed Holy Ghost accountable to the will and Word of God (pp. 21, 22).

This quotation illustrates the kind of worship experiences and priorities the church held in its early years. There was an intense desire to experience freedom in the Spirit. There was a priority placed on the Word of God. There was to be no chaotic response. There was sensitivity to the will of the Lord. And, at the same time there was to be free and individual expression by each member.

These kinds of priorities reflect the profound desire of the early Church of God members to find a spiritual fervor ever present in their lives. It was a priority. Along with educational, evangelistic and pulpit priorities, the church addressed it's spiritual priorities. Being a spiritual example was just as important as anything else done in the church.

There was a strong emphasis on unity in the early days of the Church of God. Individuals held strong convictions. This was true of the laity, pastors and leadership. However, the overriding concern was that they continue to dwell together in unity. There was a fervent call to dwell together with no divisions in the January, 1913 General Assembly. The General Overseer made the following appeal:

> The little streams and divisions must all be covered up with the flood tide of greater things. We must stand together. No division over coffee, meats etc. Look at the more important things that will save souls. Judge not in meats and drinks. I have no time to bother with such little things. God knows my heart is in this thing. Remember that in F.J. Lee's address he spoke about Paul sending men likeminded with himself who were to teach the things that he taught and nothing more. "My people are destroyed for lack of knowledge" is true today. If you want to show your ignorance just begin to cavil about things. There are a kind of stiff-necked people today like those in the time of Moses where God said, Let me alone that I may destroy them for they are a stiff necked people, but Moses fell on his face before God instead of caviling with them, and staid there until God granted his request. A set of strong men are needed today who will fall on their faces before God rather than strive and cavil over questions of no value. Let us get emptied of our own wisdom and get God's wisdom. A lot of things have not been going on as smoothly as we

would like, but we are here to heat up our irons and so apply them that all the wrinkles may be taken out. Help us Lord! Help us Lord! Help us Lord! (With great feelings and emotion.) We are going out to battle and by His grace and help we are going to do better this year than we have done in the past. These little raspings and hitchings in private conversation or in public discourses ought not to be. If you can't get such as this out of the ministry, how do you expect to get it out of the lay members and the women and children? I'm not scolding you or pointing out any one, but we must rid ourselves of these things (pp. 58-59).

These statements reflect the strong temperament of the assembly for unity. There were decisions made regarding tithing, gathering together, and so forth. However, the tone of these decisions was reflected in the above appeal. They desired to minister together in fellowship and unity. The decisions were not the consensus of any particular faction as much as the church desiring to gather together and remain together. Their commitment to oneness in the body of Christ became a foundation for continued growth and perseverance. They did not ignore the reality of divisive tendencies from time to time. But as stated above, "with great emotion," there was a constant returning to the law of love within the body of believers. This foundation kept them committed to one another as a fulfillment of their commitment to the Lord.

Another concern in the early assemblies of the church was to be accountable in their work. In the 1907 General Assembly there was a section recorded as a time of "Consecration." In the notation of this section, the ministers thought it necessary to give a testimony regarding the use of their time in the coming year. They felt accountable to the Lord and the body of Christ. As a result, the following expressions were made:

CONSECRATION

A.J. Tomlinson: "I expect to spend all my time this year in the ministry of the Word and prayer."

R.R. Spurling: "I expect to give all my time to the Lord's work this year."

Alex. Hambey: "I expect to walk in the light. When I feel that He needs me in the field I expect to go. When I feel I ought to be at home I will expect to be there, but I hold my self ready to go."

M.S. Lemons. "I expect to give all my time to the ministry of the word and prayer, but I expect to work some in garden and at home if the time is given, but if I am required to be in the work I'll let that go."

W.F. Bryant: "I expect to be in the work all the year on some line, I am at His service. I am into it with all my power. My very bones are on fire for God."

H.S. Trim: "I've been giving part of my time, I have felt I ought to give it all. If God opens up a field of labor before me I expect to go into it. I mean to go on. I expect to go, God being my helper."

S.W. Smith: "I expect to do more than I have in the past. God has blest me in many ways."

Oscar Withrow led the prayer service. He said he was ready for service all the year if God led that way by His Spirit and providences. Henry McNabb, said he and his wife were ready for the battle as the lord leads. Sister W.J. Lawson spoke briefly on the ministry of prayer (pp. 24-25).

There was also a fervent accountability about the Baptism of the Holy Ghost and spiritual gifts. The members of the early assemblies felt an obligation about the use of spiritual gifts. Early in the life of the church effectiveness was strongly tied to the responsible use of spiritual gifts. In the second General Assembly expression was made concerning the need to be use of God in the area of spiritual gifts.

GIFTS OF THE SPIRIT

H.L. McNabb: The speaker dealt with the subject in a way to show conclusively they are for us today and that we should covet earnestly the best gifts. He was followed briefly by R.G. Spurling, M.S. Lemons, W.F. Bryant, Alex Hamby, all spoke freely with the power and demonstration of the Spirit. A song, incidental, by H.L. McNabb followed in quick succession and the Spirit fell, shouts, handshaking, tears and glory in our souls (pp. 25, 26).

Themes of personal spirituality and commitment to one another were evident. There were a number of matters discussed concerning the growth and operation of the church. However, the dominant concerns were for the personal fulfillment of the individual Spirit-filled believer, along with a commitment to have no divisions within the body of believers.

CHAPTER FOUR

MORAL PURITY: ELEMENTS FOR GODLY LIVING

The previous chapter looked at the first discipleship value that results in a personal relationship with God—spiritual example. This chapter will explore various aspects of moral purity—the second of the three discipleship values of the believer that result from loving God with all your heart is moral purity.

Morality has been maligned and abused in contemporary society. Whatever a person deems "moral" is considered to be right. There is hardly any fixed meaning to the concept of morality. People use it in a political sense, a personal sense and a public sense. What is moral in today's age? How can the Christian be a moral disciple? What components make up a truly godly and moral life?

The discipleship value of moral purity can be stated as follows:

We will engage in those activities which glorify God in our body and which avoid the fulfillment of the lust of the flesh. We will read, watch and listen to those things which are of positive benefit to our spiritual well-being.

Morality for the Christian believer stems from a solid love relationship with Christ that includes at least three practices:

1. Glorifying God in our body—refraining from fleshly behavior

2. Reading, watching and listening—avoiding unbecoming books, television, movies and theatrical performances

3. Benefitting spiritual well-being—well-spent leisure, wholesome entertainment

This chapter looks at various practices that contribute to moral purity and godly living. How will the world know Christ? How will the world know the difference Christ makes in a life? Living a moral life before God should be part of the believer's lifestyle, an example of faithfulness unto God and godly living before others.

The purity of the Christian disciple is based on the foundation of Scripture. Each of the practices and discipleship values that follow are based on scriptural examples. These scriptures are presented along with suggestions for living in moral purity before the Lord.

Glorifying God in Our Body

Our body is the temple of the Holy Ghost, and we are to glorify God in our body (Romans 12:1, 2; 1 Corinthians 6:19, 20; 10:31). We are to walk in the Spirit and not fulfill the lust of the flesh (Galatians 5:16). Examples of fleshly behavior which do not glorify God are noted in

several passages of Scripture (Romans 1:24; 1 Corinthians 6:9, 10; Galatians 5:19-21; Revelation 21:8). Sinful practices which are made prominent and condemned in these scriptures include homosexuality, adultery, worldly attitudes (such as hatred, envy, jealousy), corrupt communication (such as gossip, angry outbursts, filthy words), stealing, murder, drunkenness and witchcraft. Witchcraft has to do with the practices of the occult, which are forbidden by God and lead to the worship of Satan.

Temple of the Holy Ghost. In Romans 12:1, 2, we read: "I beseech you therefore, brethren, by the mercies of God, that ye present your bodies a living sacrifice, holy, acceptable unto God, which is your reasonable service. And be not conformed to this world; but be ye transformed by the renewing of your mind, that ye may prove what is that good, and acceptable, and perfect will of God."

This passage is an appeal based on the majesty of the Lord that Paul has just described in the latter part of the previous chapter (11:33-36). It is an endeavor to apply the power of God to the believer's life through faithful commitment to Him. His work is not a mere abstraction or principle—He changes believers when they present themselves as a sacrifice. God in turn accepts the faithful sacrifice offered to Him through His Son. This acceptance transforms and changes lives. But it requires an act of personal obedience.

The body is the temple through which God's will is accomplished. The power of God operates in nature and various other manifestations. However, God has also chosen the body of the believer to further reveal His power and will. This is done primarily through the work of the Holy Spirit. The body of the believer becomes the temple of the Holy Spirit. From this position, the Holy

Spirit works to glorify the heavenly Father and carry out His will according to His Word.

> What? know ye not that your body is the temple of the Holy Ghost which is in you, which ye have of God, and ye are not your own? For ye are bought with a price: therefore glorify God in your body, and in your spirit, which are God's (1 Corinthians 6:19, 20).

This passage gives direction and purpose to the idea that the body of the believer is the "temple of the Holy Ghost." The purpose is to glorify God, not to seek personal fulfillment or even to meet the needs of others. The Holy Spirit works in the believer ultimately to glorify the heavenly Father.

Later, Paul demonstrates the extent to which we are to glorify the Lord: "Whether therefore ye eat, or drink, or whatsoever ye do, do all to the glory of God" (10:31). Glorifying God is not a mere religious exercise or ritual. The believer's entire life and practice is changed because of the indwelling power of the Holy Spirit. Again, this places the emphasis on the work of the Spirit within us, not our self-centered motives or actions.

Paul gives a straightforward admonition and command about the walk in the Spirit. "This I say then, Walk in the Spirit, and ye shall not fulfill the lust of the flesh" (Galatians 5:16).

Yielding to the Holy Spirit is part of the believer's life, especially the Pentecostal believer because it is the most effective and powerful aspect of walking in the Spirit. The alternative to not walking under the guidance and control of the Holy Spirit is to be controlled by the flesh—the corrupting, self-centered spirit of man. This too is not optional. It is automatic when the walk in the Spirit is not a reality in the believer. Then the lusts of the flesh become the fulfilling influence—guiding, leading and eventually controlling the person.

God will not force a person to be obedient to Him (see Romans 1:24). Those who do not yield to the Holy Spirit will not be part of the kingdom of God and will eventually give themselves over to various kinds of ungodly manifestations—that is, fornicators, idolaters, adulterers, effeminate, abusers of themselves with mankind, thieves, covetous, drunkards, revilers, extortioners (see 1 Corinthians 6:9, 10; Galatians 5:19-21). The final outcome of a life not yielded to the Holy Spirit but yielding to the works and lifestyle of the flesh is eternal punishment in hell (Revelation 21:8).

Additional Scriptural Insights

The work of the Holy Spirit is pivotal to the success of moral purity in a life. His Word tells us, "Grieve not the holy Spirit of God" (Ephesians 4:30). We cannot make ourselves pure before God. It takes the intervention of the Holy Spirit applying the presence and power of Christ within a life to be cleansed. Therefore, the task is not to see how pure I can become . . . my responsibility is to see how the Holy Spirit can further control me in order to allow Christ's righteousness to be operative within me.

In Ephesians 4 several specific admonitions were made. These regarded *understanding* (v. 18), *feelings* (v. 19), *lifestyle* (vv. 20-22), the *mind* (v. 23), *lying* (v. 25), *emotions* (vv. 26, 27), *stealing* (v. 28), *communication* (v. 29) and several other character traits and behaviors (vv. 31, 32).

Right in the middle of these admonitions is a call to "grieve not the holy Spirit" (v. 30). This was because the power and action of the Holy Spirit is at the very center of moral purity. This call has been used in the modern church frequently in reference to worship. This application is not in error. However, the immediate context of the passage is to matters of holiness and purity. The task of the believer is to allow, not grieve the work of the Holy Spirit in purifying him for the Lord's service.

Discipleship values should stress the central role of the Holy Spirit in matters such as prayer, Scriptural devotion, following the leading of the Spirit and allowing the Spirit to keep a person from ungodly practices. The work of the Holy Spirit should not only be stressed for worship experiences, but also for powerful, victorious living in matters of moral purity.

Another pivotal scripture in the midst of several admonitions regarding behavior is "Be filled with the Spirit" (Ephesians 5:18). The first part of Ephesians 5 addresses several commands for the Christian. These include being followers of the Lord (v. 1), walk in love (v. 2), walk as children of light (v. 8), reprove the darkness (v. 11), awake (v. 14) and walk circumspectly (v. 15).

The summary and climactic command was to be filled with the Spirit (v. 18). This command captured the essence of all the other commands. It was the foundation for the other commands. Being controlled and filled with the Spirit was the element which made the others possible.

Discipleship values in areas of moral purity must emphasize the ennoblement of the Spirit. Intellect, support from others and other factors as valuable as they may be cannot replace the role of the Spirit. The natural outcome, if believers are truly controlled by the Spirit of God, will be moral purity and the ability to fulfill the commands of the Lord.

Specific practices of the flesh. Paul not only emphasized the role of the Spirit but he also specified character
traits and actions that were indicative of life in the Spirit.
The modern-day pastor can learn from this lesson by
Paul. Effective discipleship values in the area of moral
purity must specify the traits and actions that reflect the
Spirit-filled walk. It is ineffective and does not help individuals, even spiritually, when behaviors, attitudes and
actions for moral purity are not specified. Not only will
the actions necessary for effective living not be manifested, but the spiritual condition of the person will also
begin to wane.

Some examples of the traits and actions Paul specified
as being indicative of the absence of the power of the
Spirit in a life included the following: adultery, fornication, uncleanness, lasciviousness, idolatry, witchcraft,
hatred, variance, emulation, wrath, strife, sedition, here-
sies, envying, murders, drunkenness and reveling
(Galatians 5:19-21). Examples of traits reflective of a
life yielded to the Spirit included the following: love
thy neighbor as thyself, joy, peace, longsuffering, gentleness, goodness, faith, meekness and temperance
(vv. 14, 22, 23).

Guarding against witchcraft. The practical commitments mention the area of witchcraft and effective discipleship values give attention and watchfulness to this
area. It is a very contemporary problem. There are
varieties of degrees of manifestations of witchcraft.
Some are more subtle than others. They include slight
references to demons and spirits, all the way to open
practices of the occult. Because of the increasing inter-
est in spiritual things, it is incumbent for us to clarify the
reality of the Spirit of God as opposed to false and
demonic spirits.

Reading, Watching and Listening

The literature we read, the programs we watch and the music we listen to profoundly affect the way we feel, think and behave. It is imperative, then, that the Christian read, watch and listen to those things which inspire, instruct and challenge to a higher plane of living. Therefore, literature, programs and music which are worldly in content or pornographic in nature must be avoided. A Christian is not to attend (or watch on television) movies or theatrical performances of a demoralizing nature (Romans 13:14; Philippians 4:8).

In Romans 13:14, the apostle says, "But put ye on the Lord Jesus Christ, and make not provision for the flesh, to fulfill the lusts thereof." Walking in the Spirit is an act whereby the believer submits to Christ and at the same time resists the influence of the flesh. The power of Christ enables the believer to do both, but the role of the believer is to yield to Christ and be obedient to Him. This obedience and yielding to Him results in being clothed with Christ and able to resist the works of the flesh.

The word *provision* comes from the Greek word *pronoia*, and means to place something in front of you or your mind. The corresponding term in verse 14 is *lusts*. It is the response, the provision that leads to lust.

The importance of this verse to the area of what the believer reads, watches or listens to is that the material may represent a "provision"—something that is not in accord with God's Word, and guidance of the Holy Spirit. The end result of such provision is lust of the flesh. The process is inevitable to those who are not in tune with the Spirit.

Philippians 4:8 is the foundation for living in moral purity: "Finally, brethren, whatsoever things are true, whatsoever things are honest, whatsoever things are just, whatsoever things are pure, whatsoever things are lovely, whatsoever things are of good report; if there be any virtue, and if there be any praise, think on these things."

A major review of this passage is given in chapter 1. Paul presents himself as having been able to carry out these components when he admonished them to follow Him in these areas in verse 9. The key to being able to do them for Paul and the other believers was the work of Christ within them.

Additional Scriptural Insights

Impact on feelings. Much of the power of the media today is the impact it has on desires and affections. The visual media is attuned to the sensations and responses that can be evoked emotionally from a person. Effective discipleship development must be aware of the emotional impact of the media. The content of a movie or video may not be nearly as life changing as its emotional impact. Christian media can also be used as a positive and godly tool to counteract the emotional impact of worldly media.

Impact on thinking. An individual's thinking is also changed by media experiences and a pastor does well to address these potential changes. The impact on the mind by the media is primarily the long-term effect of constant exposure to a certain theme. If a message is heard or seen long enough, it will more than likely change a person's thinking to the extent that it will be difficult to reverse.

Effective discipleship values in areas of moral purity should emphasize the dangers of long-term media exposure that affect lifestyle changes. Believers should be aware of these effects and counteract them by providing alternative messages on a regular basis. For example, messages about priorities of the family must be given repeatedly because of the constant barrage by the media about the breakdown of the family. Changes in mind and attitude are a matter of routine, habit and regular exposure.

Impact on behavior. Behaviors are modeled and mimicked. When persons hear a message long enough to become emotionally hooked and change their thinking about traditionally held beliefs and principles, these changes will eventually be displayed in their behavior. Pastoral warnings, along with specifying the kinds of behavior that in turn make for moral purity, are important.

Benefitting Spiritual Well-Being

The use of leisure time in the life of a Christian should be characterized by those activities which edify both the individual and the body of Christ (Romans 6:13; 1 Corinthians 10:31, 32). We are to avoid places and practices which are of this world. Consequently, a Christian must not be a part of any other types of entertainment which appeal to the fleshly nature and/or bring discredit to the Christian testimony (2 Corinthians 6:17; 1 Thessalonians 5:21, 22; 1 John 2:15-17).

Leisure affects every aspect of a person—mind, heart, body and spirit. What a person chooses for recreation and relaxation reflects his or her priorities. The thoroughness of yielding all of who we are was stressed by Paul when he exhorted the Romans to not "yield ye your members" to unrighteousness (Romans 6:13; see also 1 Corinthians 10:31, 32). He was stressing how the commands of Christ should infiltrate every part of their lives. Further, he admonished the Corinthians that regardless of the habits or practices of a believer, "whether therefore ye eat, or drink, or whatsoever ye do," should be done committed to the Lord.

Entertainment. Passages in 2 Corinthians 6:17; 1 Thessalonians 5:21, 22 and 1 John 2:15-17 convey principles that should guide the Pentecostal believer's selection of entertainment. Other passages in this section stress the importance of the guidance of the Holy Spirit and specify some of the principles the Spirit uses in giving that direction.

Believers are to stay away from those things, places and individuals that influence and direct them away from the cleanliness of God (2 Corinthians 6:17). God's Word and the direction of His Spirit determine the purity of God in believers' lives and are not centered around the needs of individuals.

The believer is to "prove" or test things, individuals and circumstances to see whether they are of God (1 Thessalonians 5:21). We cannot be passive, simply waiting for some compelling reason to abstain from evil forms of entertainment. The Pentecostal believer must discern the intent and content of any entertainment to see if it is of God or not.

Believers must remove themselves from the "appearance" of evil. *Appearance* comes from the Greek word *eidos*. It stresses the observation and characteristics of something. In other words, if something is characteristically evil and known to be such, the believer should "abstain," that is, keep away from such things, persons or circumstances. The consequences and eventual results have been discussed earlier in this chapter.

First John 2:15-17 stresses that giving in to the influences of the world and correspondingly moving away from the control of the Spirit has lasting consequences. Choices about entertainment are not just about immediate gratification or even fulfillment—they are about eternal commitments and destiny. Entertainment can be the battleground that solidifies a person's relationship with Christ or it can be the eroding factor that will eventually rob someone of heaven.

Additional Scriptural Insights

The concept of "edifying." Edification is a barometer of the effectiveness of a person's Christian walk. Believers are encouraged to not only ponder those behaviors that are edifying (see Philippians. 4), but they are encouraged to edify others through their actions (see Ephesians 4). Even in worship, believers were to be sensitive and edifying toward others (see 1 Corinthians 14). Moral purity can be communicated through the disciplines of personal and interpersonal edification. If it is good for others and ourselves in the Lord, it will be morally pure before Him.

Edification in the Greek text meant to "build up, to enhance someone." The word depicts the assistance of an individual in accomplishing goals and achievements that are helpful to them. The very nature of godly, moral purity is edifying. Disciples must emphasize that moral purity is not a negative principle, but rather one which will help the believers accomplish their goals and achievements that the Lord has for them.

The role of community. Another important theme for moral purity is Christian community. Not only is the direction of the Holy Spirit required for pure living, the interaction with other believers in the body of Christ is also necessary. The character of godly purity is demonstrated in the midst of relationships, not in isolation.

Effective development of discipleship values should include programs and concepts that demonstrate the necessity of fellowship for purity. Some in a congregation might be tempted to take a "lone ranger" mentality about holiness. They might think that they do not need anyone to tell them how to be morally pure, nor do they think they need anyone's help. This kind of exclusivism can be detrimental to themselves and others.

Application

The principles of moral purity must not be ivory-tower concepts, given only to thought and reflection. They must become motives and actions that direct the life of the believer. In order to apply the principles discussed in this chapter, the following suggestions are made:

1. Realize that the power to overcome the flesh and provisions for the lust of the flesh comes from Christ. Christians must seek to develop stamina in resisting temptation as they yield to the power available through the Holy Spirit.

2. Become spontaneous and decisive in staying away from the "provisions" for the lust of the flesh.

3. Realize that no one forces you to yield to the lusts of the flesh. What Satan does is try to place in front of you the occasion and opportunity for you to decide to yield to temptation.

4. Remove yourself, not only from the temptation, but also from the path and occasion for temptation.

CHAPTER FIVE

PERSONAL INTEGRITY: SHOWING FORTH THE CHARACTER OF CHRIST

Faith and victorious living are outgrowths of the presence of personal integrity. If personal integrity has been properly emphasized, godly living will follow. On the other hand, if personal integrity is absent, the development of Christian maturity is difficult, if not impossible.

Success and failure in life may be judged in different ways but personal integrity is a primary way of judging a believer's true success before God. Personal integrity is the ability to place priority on our inner, spiritual life and then integrate that into our external behavior. The two are inseparable. Integrity is first formed in the heart. It is then exemplified in our actions.

The discipleship value of personal integrity is stated in the Practical Commitments:

We will live in a manner that inspires trust and confidence, bearing the fruit of the Spirit, and seeking to manifest the character of Christ in all our behavior.

There are three basic practices that illustrate what it means to be a person of personal integrity—trust and confidence, the fruit of the Spirit and the character of Christ. Each of these covers several fundamental topics related to the development and maintenance of personal integrity.

Trust and Confidence

A Christian should be trustworthy, dependable, and a person of his word (Matthew 5:37; 1 Peter 2:11, 12). Therefore, the swearing of oaths is contrary to a Christian's trustworthiness and should be avoided (Matthew 5:34-37; James 5:12). Christ, by precept and example, taught that we love our enemy and prefer our brother (Matthew 5:43-48; Romans 12:10; Philippians 2:3; 1 John 3:16). We should behave in a way that will point others to Christ (Matthew 5:16; 1 Corinthians 11:1).

Trust and confidence is the first practice of personal integrity. Dependability is a manifestation of the Spirit of truth (John 14). The believer cannot be one person today and another tomorrow. The Christian cannot say one thing and then do another. Consistency of character is foundational for building integrity. Nothing erodes the character of the Christian like a lack of truth. The erosion may be small at first, but even at the slowest pace, the crevices erode the Christian's character until it collapses.

Being trustworthy. In Matthew 5:34-37, Jesus presents the message of trustworthiness as part of the Sermon on the Mount. He addressed the subject by warning against swearing. The Lord admonished that our conversation and deeds be done in straightforward honesty before God. Believers are not to place the fate or credibility of what they say or do on anything else except truthfulness before God. The same kind of exhortation is given in James 5:12.

Peter says that truthfulness is especially important when there is resistance to truthfulness (2:11, 12). Honest works in the name of the Lord, despite opposition, are a witness to the glory of God.

Loving our enemy and preferring our brother. In Matthew 5:43-48, Jesus said our response to enemies must be love, blessing and prayer. These mark the believer as a child of God. As the Father loved, so should His children love—even their enemies. John's admonition is similar in 1 John 3:16, that is, the love of God is revealed to others as we extend His love toward even those who are against us.

Esteeming others. Paul admonished the Philippian believers to have a mind-set that esteems others better than themselves (Philippians 2:3). The motivation was Christ's own example. He was obedient unto death for the sake of the salvation of others (Philippians 2:1-13). Preferring others is a very devout and honorable attitude (Romans 12:10) that demonstrates faith in Christ and His work on the Cross.

John was perhaps more emphatic than Paul about esteeming others. He described it as "laying down our lives" (see 1 John 3:16). As Christ laid down His life, believers must also lay down their lives for others. John felt this was an effective way to demonstrate the love of Christ.

Behavior that points to Christ. Witnessing to others includes our behavior. Specific actions make the gospel real to others. In Matthew 5:16, one of the first principles Jesus declared in the Sermon on the Mount was that a person's "good works" glorify God. These works are actually an extension of God's work within the believer that

Jesus called the "light." Refusing to subject our behavior to the Lord means that God's desire to work through us is stifled. Furthermore, the Father will not receive glory and the declaration of the gospel will be hindered. It is important for our behavior to model Christ to others. In 1 Corinthians 11:1 Paul encouraged others to follow his example. Believer should not be ashamed of or compromising about their behavior.

Fruit of the Spirit

If we live in the Spirit, we will manifest the fruit (attitudes and actions) of the Spirit and will not fulfill the lusts of the flesh (Galatians 5:16, 22-25; 1 John 1:7). Trustful relationships with others are a natural outgrowth of our positive relationship with the Lord (Psalm 1:1-3; Matthew 22:37-40). A lack of fruit-bearing in our lives will be judged (Matthew 7:16-20; Luke 13:6-9; John 15:1-8).

Bearing the fruit of the Spirit indicates the presence of personal integrity. Just as a genuine fruit tree bears fruit, the presence of the Spirit in the life of the believer bears fruit that is pleasing to God. Just as earthly fruit has aroma, flavor and productivity, so does the life of a Christian who allows the Holy Spirit to work the will of the Father.

Believers must live lives that display their reliance on God. The concept of "fruit" means that their behavior is the result of a condition within. That condition is a fellowship with Christ that cleanses and gives power for godly living (see 1 John 1:7). Those who depend on God will display the work of the Spirit within (see Galatians 5:16-18).

Paul listed the works of the flesh in Galatians 5:19-21. The following is a table of definitions for these behaviors:

Word	Definition
Adultery	Marital infidelity
Fornication	Premarital sexual activity
Uncleanness	Lack of spiritual and physical purity
Lasciviousness	Shocking and uncontrolled living
Idolatry	Serving other gods besides the Lord
Witchcraft	Using illegal drugs and practicing magic
Hatred	Hostility toward others
Variance	Habitual strife against others
Emulation	Consumed with jealousy
Wrath	Anger and hot temperedness
Strife	Seeking self-gain
Sedition	Going against others to divide them
Heresy	Creating false doctrines and divinations
Envying	Desiring and striving to possess something that is someone else's
Murder	Wrongful slaying of another
Drunkenness	Under the influence of alcohol
Revelling	Strong desire for uncontrolled pleasure with others

By contrast, Paul listed nine character traits that result from the Spirit-filled life. The following table lists these:

Word	Definition
Love	Love of God within us for others
Joy	Joy based on a relationship with God
Peace	Being whole and complete in God
Longsuffering	The ability to persevere because of God's strength
Gentleness	Responding with God's tenderness when tempted to be harsh
Goodness	Having godly character
Faith	Ability to believe because of Christ within
Meekness	Christlike gentleness and submissiveness
Temperance	Self-discipline motivated by a desire for Christlikeness

Relationships with the Lord. As mentioned earlier, the ability to be Christlike in character and behavior comes from a relationship with the Lord. The believer's walk is not guided by the works of darkness, but by a desire for God (Psalm 1:1-3). Furthermore, love for our neighbor is rooted in our love for God (Matthew 22:37-40). A lack of godly behavior or character traits is a serious reflection of the person's walk with the Lord.

Fruit will be judged. The Bible lists serious consequences for those who do not bear the fruit of the Spirit. The works that do not reflect the fruit of the Spirit will be cut out and cast into eternal punishment (see Matthew 7:16-20). Jesus displayed a decisive attitude toward unfruitfulness (see Luke. 13:6-9). He taught that unfruitfulness and bearing ungodly fruit was a direct indication of the absence of a living relationship with Him (see John 15:1-8).

Character of Christ

Love for others is the hallmark of the Christ-life (John 13:34, 35; 15:9-13; 1 John 4:7-11). In His relationship with His Father, Jesus displayed submission (Luke 22:42; John 4:34; 5:30). In His relationship with others, He demonstrated acceptance (John 8:11), compassion (Matthew 9:36; Mark 6:34), and forgiveness (Matthew 9:2; Luke 5:20). We cannot bear the fruit of the Spirit and manifest the character of Christ without being spiritually joined to Christ (John 15:4, 5) and without having the seed of the Word planted in our heart (John 15:3; 1 Peter 1:22, 23).

Ultimately, a Christian's personal integrity will reveal the character of Christ. The flow of the presence of Christ in the believer attests to the reality of Christ. Christ is glorified through His disciples. His character is manifest through Christians who genuinely possess personal integrity. The believer must practice the presence and character of Christ to fulfill the walk of personal integrity.

Love for others. Love is the identifying characteristic of Christlikeness in the body of Christ (see John 13:34, 35). This is the commandment Christ made to the disciples as He neared the Cross. It is a lesson and message that remained with John. In the latter portion of his ministry, John still taught the importance of Christlike love between believers (1 John 4:7-11).

Submission. Submission was at the heart of Christ's sacrifice on the cross (see Luke 22:42). Even though it was not easy, Christ died in order to be submissive to the will of the Father. He taught His disciples that their lives and ministries depended on being submissive to the will of the Father (see John 4:34). Christians' lives are not their own. They must be submissive to the will of the Father.

79

Acceptance. Christ also displayed an attitude of acceptance. No matter how great the sin, forgiveness is always possible for the repentant sinner. The woman caught in adultery was guilty of a grave sin. Nevertheless, Christ taught and exercised forgiving acceptance and commissioned her to live a life free from sin (see John 8:11).

Compassion. Compassion also marks the character of Christ. Christ knew the wayward condition of others. This was the reason He called laborers (see Matthew 9:36). His compassionate perception of the condition of others moved Him to teach and minister to them (see Mark 6:34). The believer must be moved by compassion, which is the initial step in ministry perception, calling and action.

Forgiveness. Christ's concern for forgiveness was demonstrated by the priority He placed on a person's relationship with the Father. While healing the man with palsy, Jesus was concerned about his spiritual condition (see Matthew 9:2; Luke 5:20). Ministry to the physical could not be separated from the spiritual. Forgiveness is the catalyst for this priority.

Being joined to Christ. Believers must live in such a way that others will see Christ living in them. This requires a strong, ongoing relationship with the Lord. John 15:4, 5 describes this relationship like a branch that depends on a vine for nourishment and life. Without the strong, vibrant connection of life, the vine could "do nothing" (v. 5).

Word planted in a heart. Peter taught that the Word was the connection between love for God and love for others in the body of Christ (see John 15:3). The Word makes this love possible in the first place. Then this love for God and others begins to flourish. Personal integrity before God and others is not a human virtue—it is the natural result of a real and vibrant relationship of love natural result of a real and vibrant relationship of love and dependence on God.

Additional Insights

Calling and unity. Calling refers to the fact that the believers are not living lives they have chosen themselves—God has called them to service. *Unity* refers to the way integrity is lived in the context of Christian community. Christian love in the church was the context in which personal integrity and the church flourished in the New Testament.

In Ephesians 4, Paul emphasized both the calling and unity of the believer in verse 1. He then discussed the characteristics of the walk that should accompany the call. These characteristics relate integrity issues to ministry and the church. Later he talked about gifts and offices in the church (v. 11). However, this is only possible because of the foundation of personal integrity already discussed in verses 2 and 3.

Characteristics of the walk of integrity. Ephesians 4:2, 3 outlines this walk: "With all lowliness and meekness, with longsuffering, forbearing one another in love; Endeavoring to keep the unity of the Spirit in the bond of peace." The life of the church is directly correlated to the integrity of individual believers. The pastor must be concerned not only for the strength of the overall church, but with the strength of individuals.

In the first part of verse 2, Paul describes a three-fold walk. First, it is to be with "all lowliness." *Lowliness* in the Greek text means humility in heart or understanding. In this verse the word refers to subjecting "oneself to others and to be more concerned about their welfare than one's own" (Walter Grundmann, *Theological Dictionary of the New Testament, VIII,* pp. 21, 22).

The second description of the kind of walk the believer is to follow is *meekness,* which comes from a Greek word meaning "mile." In this context it means "the humble and gentle attitude which expresses itself in a patient submissiveness to offense, free from malice and desire for revenge" (*Linguistic Key to the Greek New Testament,* p. 530).

The final description of the kind of walk believers are to follow is *long-suffering.* This word in Greek is constructed from two Greek words that mean "long, length" and "rush, rage." It refers to a person's long endurance in the face of raging opposition and anger from others. After this three-fold description, Paul connects these requirements for individuals with the call of the Lord to the church.

The context of personal integrity, unity with God and the church. Ephesians 4:4-6 says, "There is one body, and one Spirit, even as ye are called in one hope of your calling; One Lord, one faith, one baptism, one God and Father of all, who is above all, and through all, and in you all." This is how, after discussing personal integrity in verses 2 and 3 and before he discusses the gifts and operation of the church beginning in verse 11, Paul tells them that unity with God and the church is required. He exhorts the believers to walk in unity with God and other believers. The principles of the Christian walk are lived out in our relationships. The goals of the individual believer are connected with the life of the local body of believers.

This unity with other believers is vitally connected to unity with God. Christ prayed in the Garden of Gethsemane that the believers would be one and that they may also be one with Him (see John 17). This is the essence of Paul's exhortation here. The goal of the Christian walk is achieved through oneness with God and other believers as well. It is toward this end that Paul introduces the topic of spiritual gifts and offices.

Church of God Historical Review

This section looks at various portions of the early minutes that emphasize personal integrity. The discussions and decisions that follow reflect a desire to be led by the Holy Spirit as individuals, ministers, laity and as the church as a whole.

The General Assembly of the Church of God dealt with issues of trust and confidence. An example is the manner in which a trustworthy life was required of ministerial applicants. The presentation of the teachings of the church and the questions for ministerial applicants first appeared in the 12th issue of the church's official paper, *The Evening Light and Church of God Evangel* (Aug. 15, 1910, Vol. 1 Num. 12). It was later called *Church of God Evangel.*

A committee had been authorized in the 1909 General Assembly to investigate the matter of ministerial examination (1909 *General Assembly Minutes*, pp. 42, 43). The task of examining ministers continued with the appointment of a similar committee in the 1910 General Assembly (1910 *General Assembly Minutes*, pp. 47, 49). The report of the work by these committees was first printed in the 1910 *Church of God Evangel.*

The following is the material as it appeared in that issue:

The Church of God stands for the whole Bible rightly divided. The New Testament as the only rule for government and discipline. Below is given some of the teaching that is made prominent:

TEACHING

1. Repentance: Mark 1:15, Luke 13:3, Acts 3:19
2. Justification: Rom. 5:1, Titus 3:7
3. Regeneration: Titus 3:5
4. New Birth: John 3:3, 1, 1 Peter 1:23, 1 John 3:9
5. Sanctification subsequent to justification: Rom. 5:2, 1 Cor. 1:30, 1 Thes. 4:3, Heb. 13:12
6. Holiness: Luke 1:75, 1 Thes. 4:7, Heb. 12:14
7. Water Baptism by Immersion: Matt. 28:19, Mark 1:9-10, John 3:22, 23, Acts 8:36-38
8. Baptism with the Holy Ghost subsequent to cleansing: the enduement of power for service: Matt. 3:11, Luke 24:49-53, Acts 1:4-8
9. The speaking in tongues as the evidence of the baptism with the Holy Ghost: John 15:26, Acts 2:4, Acts 10:44-46, Acts 19:1-7
10. The full restoration of the gifts to the church: 1 Cor. 12:1-7; 10-28-31, 1 Cor. 14:1
11. Signs following believers: Mark 16:17-20, Rom. 15:18-19, Heb. 2:4
12. Fruits of the Spirit: Rom. 6:22, Gal. 5:22-23, Eph. 5:9, Phil. 1-11
13. Divine healing provided for all in the Atonement: Ps. 103:3, Isa. 53:4-5, Matt. 8:17, Isa. 5:14-16, 1 Pet. 2:24
14. The Lord's Supper: Luke 22:17-20, 1 Cor. 11:23-26
15. Washing the saints' feet: John 13:4-17, 1 Tim. 5:9-10
16. Tithing and giving: Gen. 14:18-20, Gen. 28:20-22, Mal. 3:10, Luke 11:42, 1 Cor. 16:2, 2 Cor. 9:6-6, Heb. 7:4-9-21
17. Restitution where possible: Matt. 3:8, Luke 19:9

18. Pre-millennial second coming of Jesus; First, to resurrect the dead saints, and to catch away the living saints to meet Him in the air: Matt. 24, 27-28, 1 Cor. 15:51-52, 1 Thes. 4:15-17. Second, to reign on the earth a thousand years: Zech. 14:1, 1 Thes. 4:14, 2 Thes. 1:7-10, Jude 14:15, Rev. 5:10, Rev. 19:11-21, Rev. 20:4-6

19. Resurrection: John 5:28-29, Acts 24:15, Rev. 20:5-6

20. Eternal life for the righteous: Matt. 25:46, Luke 18:30, John 10:28, Rom. 6:22, 1 John 5:11-13

21. Eternal punishment for the wicked. No liberation, nor annihilation: Matt. 25:41-46, Mark 3:29, 2 Thes. 1:8-9, Rev. 20:10-15, Rev. 21:8

22. Total abstinence from all liquor or strong drinks: Prov. 20:1, Prov. 23:29-32, Isa. 28:7, 1 Cor. 5:11, 1 Cor. 6:10, Gal. 5:21

23. Against the use of tobacco in any form, opium, morphine, etc.: Isa. 55:2, 1 Cor. 10:31-32, 2 Cor. 7:1, Eph. 5:3-8, Jas. 1:21

24. Meats and drinks: Rom. 14:2, 3-17, 1 Cor. 8:8, 1 Tim. 4:1-5

25. The Sabbath: Hosea 2:11, Rom. 14:5-6, Col. 2:16-17, Rom. 13:1-2.

EXAMINATION QUESTIONS FOR CANDIDATES FOR THE MINISTRY-EXPERIENCES AND QUALIFICATIONS.

1. Have you been baptized by immersion?

_____

2. Have you been baptized with the Holy Ghost?

_____

3. Have you spoken in tongues as the Spirit gave utterance? _____

4. Are you free from the use of tobacco in any form? _____

5. Are you free from any connection whatever with lodges or secret orders? _____

6. Have you any unpaid debts? _____

7. If so, do you see your way out? _____

8. What is your age? _____

9. How long have you lived a sanctified life?

_____

10. How long have you lived the Spirit filled life?

_____

Examination for Bishops and Deacons should be made very carefully from the rules given in 1 Tim. 3, also 1 Tim. 4:12, and Titus 1:6-9. No one need apply for the ministry who is living with a woman as his wife who is divorced, neither if he is divorced if the parties divorced from are either one living. Give the names of two devout men who are acquainted with your every day life at home and abroad. 1 Tim. 3:10, 1 Tim. 4:12. Note.The above is submitted by the committee chosen by the General Assembly which met in January, 1910. Ministers should preserve this copy of the *Evangel* for future reference (*The Evening Light and Church of God Evangel*, August 15, 1910, 1:12, p. 3).

Doctrinal adherence was not the only criterion. The concern for personal integrity also included evidence of the fruit of the Spirit in a godly life. Sam Perry of London, Kentucky described this life in a sermon, reprinted at length in the 1912 *General Assembly Minutes*. The title of the sermon was "The Deeper Life." The initial text was John 10:10, "The thief cometh not, but for to steal, and to kill, and to destroy: I am come that they might have life, and that they might have it more abundantly."

In the sermon, Sam C. Perry spoke on the believer's life in God. This "deeper life" included godly virtues of personal integrity. He gave some of the following descriptions of this "deeper life:"

We are not only called to salvation, sanctification and the baptism of the Holy Ghost, but there are greater things ahead-the fullness of Jesus Christ; it is far beyond the baptism of the Holy Ghost. . . . This wonderful truth will begin to widen out as you study the Word, and after a while we will become amazed at the magnitude of this life that we were leaving behind. . . "(1912 *General Assembly Minutes*, p. 27).

Sam C. Perry continued by describing several aspects of the "deeper life." His text for these points was 2 Peter 1:4. The point is the leaders in the early church felt that personal integrity and the fruits of living for the Lord were essential. These descriptions give some insight into their perception of the fruit of a godly life:

Partakers of the divine nature. We can be in such close contact with Him that His nature becomes a part of us; but notice, it is only upon the condition that we escape the corruption that is in the world. . . . Faith is never idle. It is always grasping after greater things. . . . Add to your faith virtue. I used to think virtue meant right living or moral excellence, but I have since found it means "excel in righteousness," or the state of being subject to Jesus. . . . To virtue, knowledge, which means to get hold of the truth, and when we do, we will know it (1912 *General Assembly Minutes,* p. 28).

Perry continued with other descriptions. He called patience "that power to be able to move along steadily." He compared it to a train staying on its tracks.

I have ridden on little sidelines where the track was uneven. The train would puff and make a frightful noise, as if going at the rate of one hundred miles an hour. The coaches swayed and rocked, and it looked as if any moment it would jump the track, but when we got on the main line much greater space was covered and in less time, while the train moved steadily along. God wants us to be on the main line (1912 *General Assembly Minutes,* p. 28).

The church felt that to emulation of the character of Christ was very important. As mentioned in the Perry sermon, there were a number of character traits that were emphasized. As Perry mentioned, righteousness was being subject to Christ.

One Christ-centered virtue that was especially emphasized was love for one another. An example is the following exhortation by the General Overseer in the 1914 General Assembly:

I feel that we have gone a million miles already in love. Some have felt more of the power of God in their bodies than ever before. We have not yet attained to entire perfection, but thank God we have gone as far as we have (*1914 General Assembly Minutes,* p. 20).

The pace for an emphasis on love had already been set by one of the founding fathers, R.G. Spurling, in the January, 1913 General Assembly (a second assembly was held in November of 1913). He described love as the element the church had lost in ages past. Now the Church of God had been able to recapture it. He described the law of love as the foundational rails upon which the church must travel. He said, "One of these golden rails represents the law, 'Thou shalt love the Lord thy God with all thy heart' and the other, 'Thou shalt love thy neighbor as thy self'" (January, 1913 *General Assembly,* p. 40).

Spurling continued in the message by saying that creeds that did not depend upon love or the Holy Ghost were like sidetracks, separate from the rails of love. He called these other tracks "narrow gauge." This was steel of a smaller measurement used for smaller locomotives. He declared the law of love to be the only rail that was the proper size. It was the only set of rails upon which the church as a locomotive, powered by the Holy Ghost, could truly travel. He also said that other rails were made of wood. He said the following about other rails or divisions:

> Here in this division they left the golden rails of the law of love and made their own rails of wood upon which the heavenly train could not run as they were narrow gauge. . . . There had been so much rubbish piled upon these golden rails through fifteen centuries of time that I have spent many sleepless nights trying to remove the rubbish and uncover these same beautiful golden rails (January, 1913 General Assembly, p. 40).

The early Church of God *General Assembly Minutes* reflect a church strongly committed to personal integrity. They felt that true religion was revealed in changed behavior.

CHAPTER SIX

THE RELATIONAL LIFE OF THE BELIEVER: LIVING FOR CHRIST WITH OTHERS

A nd the second is like unto it, Thou shalt love thy neighbour as thyself" (Matthew 22:39). With those words Jesus said that just loving God is not enough (vv. 37, 38). Loving one's neighbor is required just as much. That can be uncomfortable for people who say, "I can love God, but I have trouble loving people."

It is hard to love some people because they can be mean and hurtful. Many times people are hypocritical. How do you love these kinds of people? Your worst enemy may be in your own family. The next three chapters describe how the Christian's experience becomes more valuable, more enriched, by obeying the second great commandment of Jesus, love your neighbor as you love yourself (see Matthew 22:37-40).

The Biblical Foundation for Loving Others

There are scripture passages from the Old and New Testaments that instruct the believer in establishing values for loving others. The Old Testament passage, Leviticus 19, is from the Book of the Law. It is representative of many texts in the Law that address the importance of loving our neighbor. Four passages in the New Testament—Matthew 22, Galatians 6 and Romans 1 and 13—give practical instruction about loving others. These passages look at the general command to love those around us, giving specific directions for carrying out the command.

Commanded to Love Others

Love for neighbors. In Leviticus 19:13, 18 we read,

> Thou shalt not defraud thy neighbour, neither rob him: the wages of him that is hired shall not abide with thee all night until the morning. . . . Thou shalt not avenge, nor bear any grudge against the children of thy people, but thou shalt love thy neighbor as thyself: I am the Lord.

These verses are found in the section of Leviticus that deals with daily living (19:1-37). They come at the end of a larger section (11:44—19:37) that deals with applying holiness to various aspects of life. Relationships with others concludes the section. Personal purity and holiness in all aspects of life depend a great deal on our attitude toward others. This is why the concept of loving our neighbor summarized so many areas of holiness in this section of Leviticus.

Verse 13 emphasizes not using a position in life to abuse others. It pictured an employer who might withhold wages because of a lack of love. Even though the employer has a position of authority, this authority must not be used against another person.

Defrauding is a word that means "to oppress" or "take advantage" of someone at a cost to the other person.

Neighbor is a simple Hebrew word that means "fellowman" or "other person." The root idea of the word is *person*. This is interpreted in Old Testament history as fellow countryman. However, Jesus clarified the word to mean anyone who was around us (Luke 10:25-37).

Several passages in the New Testament, including Matthew 22:37, 38, Galatians 5:14, James 2:8, Matthew 19:19 and Romans 13:9 refer to Leviticus 19:13. It is cited as one of the most important commands in all the Law. In fact, Christ taught that it was the second most important commandment.

In Leviticus 19:18, the first concept of loving one's neighbor is used in relationship to bearing a grudge. Next, we are reminded of God's lordship. The call to love our neighbor is the opposite of bearing a grudge. Continuing to harbor resentment or attempting to gain revenge was the first emphasis of verse 18. The desire for revenge will permeate many areas of a persons life, including physical and mental health and the stability of relationships with others. The godly attitude is to transform the resentment into godly love.

The ability to love others does not come from being able to love oneself. Loving self is important. However, the phrase, "I am the Lord," in verse 8 indicates the source of love for both others and self. The ability to love comes from the power and Lordship of God. His sovereign love enables us to love others with the same kind of love we love ourselves.

This paradigm of loving others as oneself, empowered by God, does not mean that a person loves self for awhile and then loves others for awhile. The concepts cannot be separated in that way. Loving others and loving self must be simultaneous.

Love for strangers. Leviticus 19:33, 34 says, "And if a stranger sojourn with thee in your land, ye shall not vex him. But the stranger that dwelleth with you shall be unto you as one born among you, and thou shalt love him as thyself; for ye were strangers in the land of Egypt: I am the Lord your God."

The emphasis of these two verses is on the relationship of the child of God with a stranger. The term *stranger* indicated someone from a different country. The concept can be expanded to include people in general who are unlike you in some way, especially if those differences place a barrier between the two of you. The Israelite was not to take advantage of that person. This passage is similar to verse 13, which talks about not abusing a person's position or status.

The stranger was to be treated as though they had been born in the same land as the Israelites, with equal privileges and opportunities. Especially important was the attitude of the Israelites. The word *vex* addressed the inner condition and response, as well as any external actions.

The reason for such a command was two-fold. As with the command in 19:18, the lordship and power of God was one reason, as indicated by the phrase, "I am the Lord your God." The other reason was the fact that they had been strangers themselves. This experience was a reminder of the need for compassion and love. The Egyptians had treated them cruelly. The child of God is to love others and not show cruelty.

No matter how great an injustice, the believer's response should be that of love, rather than abuse. Mistreatment by others should be a reminder of the command to display love rather than vengeance. Vengeance will be done, but it is in the hands of the Lord. The obligation of the believer is to love others, even those who are different (strangers).

Love for God. "Jesus said unto him, Thou shalt love the Lord thy God with all thy heart, and with all thy soul, and with all thy mind. This is the first and great commandment" (Matthew 22:37, 38).

In this section a Pharisee asked Jesus about the greatest commandment of the law? The question was perhaps a legitimate one. Some of the commandments held more weight than others, at least in their ability to summarize and integrate other commandments. The attitude of this question was not right. The Pharisee did it to tempt the Lord and find an occasion to accuse Christ. However, Christ used the question to highlight the essence of an individual's walk with God.

Jesus' response centers on the nature of the believer's relationship with God. The relationship must be rooted and grounded in love if love is to consume the very life and walk of the believer. The word *agape* is the pinnacle expression of sincere and purposeful love. It is love expressed in enduring commitment, faithfulness, and is not dependent on circumstances.

The commandment to "love the Lord your God" indicates at least three things:

- Response to God's authority

- A personal relationship with God

- Your response to this relationship

All three in combination present a description of the personal, covenant relationship between the child of God and the one true God.

Believers are to love from their heart, soul and mind. These words express various aspects of the nature of this love.

Heart is from the Greek word *kardia*, expressing the seat of consciousness and emotions. It denotes the sentiment and desire of the believer. The affections of the Christian are to be set and turned toward the Lord.

Soul is from the Greek word *psuche* and emphasizes the source of inner life and strength. The child of God should depend on the Lord for inner strength and motivation.

Mind comes from the Greek word *dianoia*, indicating the ability to think something through. The daily life and thinking process of the Christian is to be committed and centered on the Lord.

The word *all* is used to express depth of commitment. This covenant relationship requires full participation from the believer. It cannot be tentative or temporary—it must be full and complete.

The command to love God fully is the first and greatest commandment. When we love God, He gives us power and the ability to obey all the other commandments.

Simultaneous love for self and neighbor. Matthew 22:39, 40 state: "And the second is like unto it, Thou shalt love thy neighbour as thyself. On these two commandments hang all the law and the prophets."

Jesus went beyond the Pharisee's question and added another dimension to this commandment. He explained that our relationship with others is dependent on our relationship with Him.

The word *like* indicates the necessity and depth of the second commandment. This requires the same level of commitment as the first commandment.

Love is not based on emotions or circumstances—it is commanded by God. Loving our neighbor is part of a life of obedience.

All of the law and the prophets in the Old Testament could be summarized in these two commandments because they express the fundamental relationship of believers. The first and greatest is our relationship with God; the second is our relationship with others.

Guidelines for Relating to One Another

The believer's task in fulfilling the second great commandment is to live "with one another," according to God's will. The phrase *one another* is used in the Epistles and the Book of Acts to refer to relationships. Certain attributes are used in connection with this phrase to define relationships. These attributes included qualities to develop and avoid.

All of these concepts set the tone for edifying one another in the New Testament church. Christ directed His followers in John 13:34, 35 that their love for one another would be the witness that they were His disciples. Following is a description of different aspects of godly relationships, based on the use of the phrase *one another* in the New Testament.

Positive Attributes to Develop

Kind Affection. This quality emphasizes love and tenderness in relationships. The concept comes from the Greek word *philostorgos*. It is a combination of two Greek words that mean "love affection." This means the tendency of an individual is inclined toward love, affection and tenderness. This concept is mentioned in Romans 12:10.

Love. This quality emphasizes love directed by God. It is the result of the use of intelligence and comprehension, but it is centered on the purposes of God. The word used in the Greek text is *agape.* This love seeks a higher purpose than emotions. Emotions may be felt, but the focus of love is some central meaning and motivation. In relating to one another, the love of the believer is from God. We are admonished to love one another in several passages (Romans 13:8; 1 Thessalonians 4:9; 1 Peter 1:22; 1 John 3:11, 23; 4:7, 11; 2 John 1:5).

Receive. This quality emphasizes acts of kindness and love. It is the translation of the Greek word *proslambano.* The word is used in the contexts of an action such as inviting someone into your home to show kindness. They should be received as an equal or companion. By these acts you will draw closer "receiving" the person. The opposite would be to either remain at a distance or withdraw from an individual. This word is used for relationships in Romans 15:7.

Admonish. This quality emphasizes the presentation of something to another person. The word is from the Greek word *noutheteo.* It is made up of two Greek words *nous* ("mind"/"will") and *titheemi* ("to place"). It means something that is placed in front of or in the mind of another person. It may be a thought, concept or principle. The word does not indicate the creation of anything. Rather, something is disclosed to another person. We are to advise others of things that are important for them to know and consider. This is especially true of the things of God. This word was used for relationships in Romans 15:14.

Salute/Greet. This quality highlights the importance of gestures of affection. Affection is communicated through warm, tangible actions such as a kiss or embrace. This outward expression gives assurance and support to a relationship. The Greek word used for this concept is *aspazomai*. The word essentially means "union." It is used for relationships in Romans 16:16; 1 Corinthians 16:20; 2 Corinthians 13:12 and 1 Peter 5:14.

Serve. This quality denotes service and commitment to one another. Feelings and affections toward others must be communicated through appropriate and edifying acts of service. These acts will frequently relate to the physical and temporal needs of an individual. The word comes from the Greek word *douleo,* meaning "bond servant." It describes relationships where commitment and service are important. This concept in relationships was used in Galatians 5:13.

Forbear. This characteristic sustains relationships by stressing the need for resilience and flexibility. Various actions and attitudes such as forgiveness, love and endurance might be used. However, this word conveys the need to remain committed to a relationship over an extended period of time. This aspect of relationships is highlighted in Ephesians 4:2 and Colossians 3:13.

Be kind. This quality describes a gracious and pleasant attitude. It comes from the Greek word *chrestos* and means to offer kindness and assistance. A believer should always be sensitive to the needs of others and willing to help them. The term is used for relationships in Ephesians 4:32.

Forgive. This word comes from the Greek word *charizomai.* Its meaning is rooted in the idea of graciousness. It means to respond with favor toward others who may or may not request it. This quality does not condone evil or wrongdoing, but depicts a forgiving spirit, approachable to individuals. This attitude is mentioned in Ephesians 4:32 and Colossians 3:13.

Comfort/Exhort. This quality characterizes the comforting presence you offer to others. It is made up of two Greek

words, *para* ("alongside of") and *kaleo* ("to call")—
parakaleo. This word refers to calling someone to your
side and offering support. The most comforting expression
is often the mere presence and availability of the other person. This aspect of relationships is mentioned in 1 Thessalonians 4:18, Hebrews 3:13 and 10:24.

Edify. This quality means to build up another person
with a godly attitude, effective organization and timely
action. We must not be prompted by selfish or manipula-
tive motives. Our goal is to improve the quality of the
other person's life. This concept is used regarding relationships in 1 Thessalonians 5:11.

Consider. To consider others is to perceive and understand them. Rather than merely reacting to others, thought-
ful consideration of options, circumstances and implications for relationships is important. This quality is in the
Greek word *katanoeo*. It is used regarding relationships in
Hebrews 10:24.

Negative Aspects to Avoid

Negative aspects to avoid were also used in references
to relationships in the early church. These admonish-
ments also provide insight into principles about living a
morally pure life before God and others.

Judging. A judgmental attitude questions the final
authority of God. The New Testament affirmed the sovereign will and judgment of God. No individual must act
as the final authority regarding relationships. Conclusions
are always humbly subjected to the judgment of God.
This term is applied to relationships in Romans 14:13.

Devouring. This word emphasizes a self-centered
attitude that takes advantage of others and relationships.
When self-fulfillment is the sole purpose for relating to

others, meaningful relationships cannot develop. This word was applied to relationships in Galatians 5:15.

Consuming. The perpetual desire to devour something describes this word. It is different from *devour* in its duration because it is a continual, habitual condition in relationships. The word is applied to relationships in Galatians 5:15.

Provoking. This term thrives on conflict and emphasizes a challenging and combative spirit. This kind of person is not be satisfied until some controversy is started in relationships. This term was applied to relationships in Galatians 5:26.

Envying. This word refers to a selfish desire for something possessed by another person. The implications of envy can be destructive. An envious person goes to extremes to possess what belongs to another. This word is used in reference to relationships in Galatians 5:26.

Hating. To hate is to detest or despise someone else. Hate focuses on the emotions of a person and includes anger, even rage. The danger in hatred is that it can become a compulsion. It is used in reference to relationships in Titus 3:3.

Obeying the two great commandments of love form the foundation for keeping the other values and commandments of God. Chapters 2 through 5 explored values that are directly related to the Christian's love for God. Chapters 6 through 8 present the values that grow out of simultaneous love for neighbor and self. The two discipleship values that especially come from love for self and neighbor are family responsibility and behavioral temperance. Family responsibility will be the subject of chapter 7. Behavioral temperance will be presented in chapter 8.

CHAPTER SEVEN

FAMILY RESPONSIBILITY

Family responsibility is the first discipleship value that evolves from the second great commandment—love others as yourself. Family members are our closest neighbors. Whether near or far geographically, they occupy a nearness of human kinship that begins at birth and ends at death. Handling family relationships is the first line of love. We may disagree with family. We may have been hurt by family. We may have even been dismissed by family. How we respond to those family disagreements, hurts and dismissals affects other relationships that follow. The pledge to responsibility in family values is given in the following practical commitment:

We will give priority to fulfilling family responsibilities, to preserving the sanctity of marriage and to maintaining divine order in the home.

The many facets of family commitment are explored in this chapter. Family is the foundational discipleship value that involves not only relationships in the family, but also a variety of relationships, along with many other challenges. Persistently pursuing the excellence of family values rewards the disciple with a strong foundation for other relationships. Maintaining values in the home does not mean that your family relationships have been fully perfected, it means that you are asking God to mold your love for your family.

The many dimensions of family values include at least three essential practices . . .

1. Establishing the family as a priority

2. Keeping the sanctity of marriage and

3. Maintaining divine order in the home.

Each of these will be described and scriptures that relate to those practices analyzed.

Priority of the Family

The priority of the family as a practice of discipleship values is stated below:

The family is the basic unit of human relationship and as such is foundational to both society and the church (Genesis 2:18-24). The origin of the family, along with its foundational character, makes it imperative that we give priority to ministry to the family, both from a personal and corporate standpoint. The practice of Christian disciplines and virtues should begin in the home (Deuteronomy 6:6, 7). Therefore, our families should establish some pattern for family devotions and should endeavor to provide a Christian environment in the home (1 Timothy 3:3, 4; 5:8).

Family is the foundational unit of society. In Genesis 2:18-24, the origin of the first unit of society is described.

God created the family for fellowship. It was not His plan or desire for Adam to face his responsibilities alone. Creating a family is an act of leaving mother and father, and becoming a family equipped by God to fulfill His will.

Spiritual virtues begin at home. In Deuteronomy 6:5-7, the Lord instructs parents to teach His commandments to their children. In verse 5, He gave the first and greatest commandment, that we love the Lord with all our heart. No one can replace the vital function of parents teaching their children. At best, other individuals and institutions can only supplement what parents teach.

Christian environment in the home. Paul instructed Timothy (1 Timothy 3:3, 4; 5:8) on the important role of fulfilling family responsibilities. Ruling the house well was a major criterion for church leadership in 1 Timothy 3:3, 4. The word *ruling* comes from a Greek word that means "to manage and direct." Fulfilling family obligations was also an important sign of Christian maturity (5:8). In this verse Paul speaks about widows being cared for by their own family members. These family members demonstrated their maturity in the faith by the way they took care of widows in their family.

The central need of the family is spiritual. The church should especially emphasize the salvation of each member of the family. Without a firm relationship with the Lord, parents and children will lack the strong godly commitment it takes to have a Christian home.

This depth of commitment can only be reached through Christ. Salvation of each family member is necessary to make this process effective. The church should especially seek the assurance of salvation for every member of a home so that together they can seek God's direction and power.

The challenge is to apply the standards of God's Word for marriage to the demands and changing pressures of a marriage. This is only possible through the power and grace of the Lord.

In the New Testament, the system of the family was important for the life of the church. This is the reason Paul stressed the importance of family so much.

- The family of Jesus is mentioned at critical times in the Gospels (John 7:5).

- His mother is seen at the crucifixion (John 19:17-30) and in the Upper Room, along with His brothers (Acts 1:14).

- Children were a significant part of Jesus' ministry (Matthew 19:13-15).

The family was not ignored or minimized. On the contrary, it was a basic unit of the ministry of Christ and the early church.

Sanctity of Marriage

The second practice that affirms family values and responsibility is keeping the sanctity of marriage. Marriage represents God's faithfulness to His children. The faithfulness of a husband and wife to one another is an act of faith and witness in response to God's faithfulness. Therefore, breaking the solemn vows and fidelity of marriage fractures not only human relationships, but also godly devotion. The practice of keeping the sanctity of marriage as a significant part of the value of family responsibility is stated in the following practical commitment:

Marriage is ordained of God and is a spiritual union in which a man and a woman are joined by God to live together as one (Genesis 2:24; Mark 10:7). Because of the divine character of marriage, it is a lifelong commitment with the only clear biblical allowance for divorce being fornication (Matthew 5:32; 19:9).

Sexual involvement either before marriage or with someone other than the marriage partner, is strictly forbidden in Scripture (Exodus 20:14; 1 Corinthians 6:15-18). Understanding the sanctity of marriage, partners should strive to maintain a happy, harmonious and holy relationship. Should divorce occur, the church should be quick to provide love, understanding and counsel to those involved. The remarriage of divorced persons should be undertaken only after a thorough understanding of and submission to the Scriptural instructions concerning this issue (Matthew 19:7-9; Mark 10:2-12; Luke 16:18; Romans 7:2, 3; 1 Corinthians 7:2, 10, 11). Should a Christian desire to remain single, this decision should be respected and should be seen as a viable Scriptural alternative (1 Corinthians 7:8, 32-34).

Several Scriptural principles instruct us about preserving the sanctity of marriage. Those principles and key scriptures are analyzed in the next section.

Marriage is ordained by God. The divine origin of marriage is outlined in Genesis 2:24; Mark 10:6-9; and Matthew 19:4-6. More than any other person in the New Testament, Christ taught about the sanctity of marriage.

The decision and acts of a man and woman do not constitute a marriage. A marriage is a relationship that is made possible and is sustained by God's power. Jesus taught that the "ordaining" of marriage includes both the creation and sustenance of marriage.

Admonition regarding divorce, adultery and fornication. God's Word gives strong admonitions regarding sexual involvement before marriage—fornication—and after sexual involvement after marriage with someone else—adultery.

"Thou shalt not commit adultery" was not just one a-mong many principles of God's instruction—it is the foundation of God's teachings in the Law. Prohibition of adultery was one of the 10 foundational principles of all of God's teachings (Exodus 20:14).

In 1 Corinthians 6:15-18 Paul teaches that adultery and fornication corrupt the work of the Holy Spirit in the life and body of the believer. This chapter contains the well-known reference to the body as the "temple of the Holy Ghost" (6:19). The context regards sexual purity. The effectiveness of the work of the Holy Spirit in a life is greatly diminished when a person persists in sexual impurity.

Admonition regarding divorce and remarriage. Jesus responded to questions from skeptical Pharisees about the nature of marriage, divorce and remarriage. He makes three essential points in the following passages: Matthew 19:7-9; Mark 10:2-12; Luke 16:18.

1. Jesus explains the design and will of God for the husband and wife is to continue in marriage. God created the sexes for the purpose of being joined to each other in marriage. In being joined together, they are to leave their parents and cleave to one another. Once the marriage is consummated, it was not up to man to "put it asunder," that is "divide apart" (Matthew 19:6; Mark 10:9).

2. Christ responded to questions about the "bill of divorcement" (Matthew 19:7, 8; Mark 10:4, 5) found in Deuteronomy 24:1-4. Moses created the provision because of individual corruption and hardness. Divorce is not the result of God's creation and design for marriage.

3. The Lord addressed the consequences of remarriage. In both Moses' teaching and the principles He

gave in these sections, faithfulness to the original marriage is the first principle. Remarriage represents a tragic breakup of the first union. The first union was not to be dissolved simply to facilitate a second marriage. Jesus did not discuss remarriage and the law as much as Paul. Remarriage will be covered further in this chapter under Romans 7 and 1 Corinthians 7.

In addressing remarriage, two issues pertaining to divorce and remarriage were present in Moses' discourse in Deuteronomy and Jesus' teaching: uncleanness and fornication. Moses referred to the "uncleanness" of the spouse as the basis of the bill of divorcement. *Uncleanness* was a reference that included sexual purity. The hardness of the heart of one or both spouses would result in these concepts. Jesus used the word *fornication* to refer to the hardness of their hearts.

The words *fornication* and *pornography* came from the same Greek word *porneia*. The most essential root idea of *porneia* was "to sell oneself for sexual impurity." It is used to depict those who forfeit ("sell") their chastity and virginity before marriage for ungodly pleasure and lust. Though money is not exchanged for lust, chastity is often traded for lustful pleasure. Some scholars have interpreted the word *fornication* to refer to marital infidelity, but the word used most often in the New Testament is adultery.

In Romans 7:2, 3, Paul uses statements in the law to illustrate another point—the law applies to a person as long as he or she lives. As a result, believers should consider themselves "dead" to the law through faith in Christ (7:4). The example Paul uses to illustrate faithfulness to Christ is faithfulness to marriage as a lifelong obligation. The damage has already been done in lives and homes through the hardness of hearts, but the church must shepherd and care for the families broken by divorce and remarriage.

A message similar to Romans 7 is presented by Paul in 1 Corinthians 7 where he emphasized faithfulness in marriage. He turned to the theme of marriage in verse 10 after discussing the unmarried and widows (v. 8). There had been dissension in the church at Corinth about marital fidelity and its place in the midst of diverse circumstances. Into this contention, Paul affirms the godly relationship between husband and wife: "And unto the married I command, yet not I, but the Lord, Let not the wife depart from her husband: But and if she depart, let her remain unmarried, or be reconciled to her husband: and let not the husband put away his wife" (7:10, 11).

Paul cites what Jesus said in Matthew 19:1-9 regarding the will of the Father. He also addressed times when marital partners "depart" or "put away" their spouses. *Depart* is a general term for leaving a mate. *Put away* is a technical term used for actual divorce. At the time of Paul's writing, Jewish law did not give women the legal ability to "put away" their mate, so they used *depart*, a nonlegal and nontechnical term (in this case, women) for leaving a mate.

In verses 10 and 11 Paul does not condon divorce, but he admonishes them to discontinue the practice. He exhorted them to remain unmarried and be reconciled to one another. He lifted up the importance of faithfulness in marriage.

Remaining single as a viable Scriptural alternative. In 1 Corinthians 7:8, 32-34, Paul is affirming singleness as a profitable and godly option. In no way is singleness secondary to marriage. Neither is marriage secondary to singleness. God designed male and female to fulfill his will for marriage, but He calls some to singleness (Matthew 19:10-12). Paul taught that singles are not obligated to as many physical cares that might hinder certain areas of ministry (1 Corinthians 7:32-34). This does not mean that in all cases of ministry that singleness is preferred because family is indeed a strong resource for ministry (Psalm 127) and not a burden. When God does call someone to singleness, Paul is emphasizing that it carries tremendous advantage for some areas of ministry.

Additional insight on the sanctity of marriage. In 1 Corinthians 7:12-14, we read:

> But to the rest speak I, not the Lord: If any brother hath a wife that believeth not, and she be pleased to dwell with him, let him not put her away. And the woman which hath an husband that believeth not, and if he be pleased to dwell with her, let her not leave him. For the unbelieving husband is sanctified by the wife and the unbelieving wife is sanctified by the husband: else were your children unclean; but now are they holy.

The salvation of family members should be a primary goal for families. This goal should not be threatened by dissolving the marriage because of difficult family relationships. Paul appeals to the believing members of families when he says that a believing spouse should not reject the other just because of unbelief. Rather, he or she should remain faithful to the marriage.

The sanctity of marriage is that the relationship becomes a primary tool for the salvation of the unbelieving spouse. To depart from the relationship may threaten the reception of the gospel by the other partner. This does not mean that everything an unbelieving spouse does is condoned. It does encourage the believing spouse to remain faithful.

In verse 14 Paul addresses the sanctifying effect of a believing spouse or parent on unsaved mates or children. *Sanctify* in the grammar of the Greek text of this passage indicates a process that is initiated by the Lord and is continued by the believer's faithfulness and commitment to His Word. The unbelieving member receives the active work of purification from God through a believing family member. This work can be rejected, but it is present because of the faithfulness of the believer.

Calling in marriage. First Corinthians 7:15, 16 says:

> But if the unbelieving depart, let him depart. A brother or a sister is not under bondage in such cases: but God hath called us to peace. For what knowest thou, O wife, whether thou shalt save thy husband? or how knowest thou, O man, whether thou shalt save thy wife?

In these two verses Paul addressed another form of the issue of separation and divorce. The unbelieving spouse has left the believing spouse. The question now regards the commitment of the believing spouse who remained faithful to the marriage. The commitments of the remaining spouse may change. To what degree the change may take place was not made clear in the passage. At times, Paul used the word *bondage* to mean remaining in exactly the same kind of relationship. However, the nature of the bondage was not fully described.

Whether the possible change in commitments included the believer marrying someone else was not directly indicated in verse 15. The words *bondage* and *peace* are not specifically defined. But the context in which they are used has been interpreted in at least two ways. In the first interpretation, prohibition from remarrying has been interpreted as part of the bondage, leaving the remaining spouse free to remarry.

In the second interpretation, *bondage* refers to freedom from commitments and burdens, but does not give the freedom to remarry. These commitments might include where to live, financial obligations, efforts to support someone, and so forth. The remaining spouse was still committed to the context of verses 10 and 11, to remain unmarried and not divorced.

The clearest admonition is in the phrase, "Let him depart." The bondage was certainly attached to efforts to try to keep someone who is determined to leave from leaving. Paul is not advocating that the other spouse leave. He is recognizing that the faithful spouse cannot control the unfaithful spouse.

This is not an act of futility, but it is one of hope similar to Paul's admonition in 2 Timothy 2:25, 26. Paul speaks of people who are opposed to salvation but who can become aware of their pitiful condition and come to know the Lord.

Paul's appeal in 1 Corinthians 7:15 is for the restoration of the unfaithful spouse. The efforts to keep a wayward spouse from leaving may be futile; however, the call to seek reconciliation of the lost spouse must continue. The faithful never stop praying and interceding for the restoration of the lost spouse. This continued hope is the focus of verse 16.

The salvation of a lost spouse is the primary concern of Paul. Whether or not there is permission to remarry is a matter of implication or interpretation. There is a calling in marriage that never leaves—a calling to seek the salvation of both partners and children. Paul continued emphasizing this calling throughout this passage up to verse 24.

Divine Order in the Home

The third practice that affirms the disciple's values for the family is sustaining divine order in the home.

> *When God created man, He created them male and female (Genesis 1:27). He gave them distinctly different characteristics (1 Corinthians 11:14, 15; 1 Peter 3:7) as well as different responsibilities (Genesis 3:16-19; 1 Peter 3:1-7). In God's order the husband is head of the home (Ephesians 5:22-31; Colossians 3:18, 19), parents are to nurture and admonish their children (Ephesians 6:4, Colossians 3:21), and children are to obey and honor their parents (Exodus 20:12; Ephesians 6:1-3; Colossians 3:20). In order for harmony to exist in the home, God's order of responsibility must be observed.*

A number of principles and scripture passages affirm the value of God's divine order in the home. The following passages provide insight into God's order for the family.

God created male and female (Genesis 1:27; 3:16-19; 1 Corinthians 11:14-15; 1 Peter 3:7). These passages emphasize that God created the distinctions in human sexuality for the bond of marriage. The principle differences between husband and wife are not just physical. There are differences in overall functions that are not only unique individually, but also relate to whether the person is a father and husband or a mother and wife.

These passages illustrate some of those characteristics:

- Genesis 1:27 emphasizes sexual differences.

- Genesis 3:16-19 emphasizes the impact of child rearing and work.

- First Corinthians 11:14, 15 emphasizes spiritual responsibility before God.

- First Peter 3:1-8 refers to physical differences and the requirement of sharing and love. All of these characteristics mark maturity as men and women, husbands and wives and fathers and mothers.

Husband as head of the home. Ephesians 5:22-33 and Colossians 3:18, 19 point out the distinctions between the roles of husbands and wives. The role of the husband is to love his wife. The role of the wife is to recognize the leadership of her husband. The context of Ephesians 5 is godly submission; they are both to submit one to another in the fear of the Lord (v. 21). The context of Colossians 3 is living a Christ-centered life (v. 17). In other words, a husband fulfilling his role and a wife fulfilling her role exemplify the leadership and indwelling of Christ.

In Ephesians 5, Paul describes the Christian walk through a series of exhortations:

- Walk in love (v. 2).

- Walk in light (v. 8).

- Reprove darkness (v. 11).

- Awake (v. 14).

- Walk circumspectly and be wise (vv. 15-17).

- Be filled with the Spirit (v. 18).

This last exhortation is the climax of the series because it is the primary characteristic that describes the nature of the Christian walk.

Spirituality is illustrated in two ways. Verses 19 and 20 describe spirituality demonstrated in worship. The words *speaking* and *giving* are circumstantial modifiers that are used to amplify the basic exhortation to be filled with the Spirit. The largest section of Paul's discourse, 5:21—6:4, describes the application of spirituality through submissive relationships in the family. *Submitting* is also a modifier of the basic exhortation to be filled with the Spirit and applies to both husband and wife (5:21). The home is the place to submit to one another in love, reverence and obedience (5:33; 6:1).

Paul's illustration of the family in this text implies that spirituality is exhibited through godly relationships in the family. He briefly mentioned worship. However, he spent the majority of time referring to submission within the family to illustrate the importance of a Spirit-filled life.

Additional Insights

In addition to the passages cited, several additional scriptures support family values. These additional insights give further understanding to the practices already mentioned.

Emphasizing reverence in submission.

> Wives, submit yourselves unto your own husbands, as unto the Lord. For the husband is the head of the wife, even as Christ is the head of the church: and he is the saviour of the body. Therefore as the church is subject unto Christ, so let the wives be to their own husbands in every thing (Ephesians 5:22-24).

Marital and family issues must be grounded in a Biblical perspective of submission. This perspective involves submission by both marriage partners. Humility before God, submission, love and reverence were mentioned by Paul as the heart of marital relationships—not emotions, social expediency or tradition.

Emphasis on submission began in verse 21 with the phrase, "Submitting yourselves one to another in the fear of God." Out of this initial exhortation Paul called wives to emphasize reverence in their submission, and husbands to emphasize love in their submission. Both areas—reverence and love—were to be shown by both husbands and wives.

Paul does not explain why he highlighted the different areas of reverence and love. The scripture context indicated that there is a need on the part of husbands to love sacrificially as Christ sacrificed Himself for the church. Also, the context indicated that there is a need for wives to demonstrate more recognition of their husbands in the role of spiritual leader of the home.

Submitting comes from a Greek word that means to "place under authority." The use of the word by Paul means to "place oneself under the authority of another." This action is to be initiated and enacted by both husband and wife without force or coercion. Ultimately, God is the authority to which both husband and wife are to submit. This is the intention of the phrase "in the fear of God." The power and authority of God monitors the relationship between husband and wife.

The role of the husband is compared to the headship of Christ over the church. This is the emphasis of the word *head*. The function of this headship is conveyed in the word *saviour.* It is a redeeming and reconciling position. The position of the Lord and the husband is not for manipulation or abuse of power. Rather, it is to serve and reconcile through the position of leadership. Just as Christ redeemed the lost through the honor given Him, the husband is to reconcile his wife through the leadership position given him.

The wife is to recognize and respect this position and function and be *subject* to the husband. This word is similar to the word *reverence* used in verse 33, with emphasis on serving the Lord by cooperating with the husband's leadership.

Emphasizing love in submission. Ephesians 5:25, 28, 29 gives this instruction: "Husbands, love your wives, even as Christ also loved the church, and gave himself for it. . . . So ought men to love their wives as their own bodies. He that loveth his wife loveth himself. For no man ever yet hated his own flesh; but nourisheth and cherisheth it, even as the Lord the church."

The motivation and reason for a husband's love for his wife is the same as the work of Christ in behalf of the church. Before focusing on self-sacrifice, Paul highlights the results of Christ's love and self-sacrifice. This description of Christ's work parallels an earlier reference to Christ being the Savior of the body in verse 23. In a similar way, Christ's sacrifice of self results in the sanctification and cleansing of the church (v. 26) and the glorious presentation of the church before the Father (v. 27).

Self-sacrifice was emphasized in verses 28-32 as the central feature of the love a husband should have for his wife. Self-sacrifice was commanded in verse 28. Three reasons for self-sacrifice follow:

1. Nourishment (v. 29)

2. The unity of the church in Christ (v. 30)

3. Unity within marriage (v. 31)

Paul completed the section on self-sacrifice and unity in verses 28-32 by referring to the mystery of those principles. Christ displayed the ultimate answer to the mystery of self-sacrifice and unity in marriage by loving the church and giving Himself for it.

The same context for spousal roles is also used for parental nourishing. Godly submission (Ephesians 5:21) is to be displayed through parental nurture (6:4). Christ-centered living (Colossians 3:17) is to be fostered through parental care (v. 21). These passages provide instructions about avoiding provocation and anger in parenting. Persistent anger by parents causes discouragement and despair in children.

Obeying and honoring parents. Ephesians 6:1, "Children obey your parents in the Lord: for this is right," is often quoted by parents. Christian parents must also effectively address parent-child relationships in order to fully affirm the value of family responsibility. Parent-child relationships are just as important as husband-wife relationships in the home. Children are placed at the bottom of the priority lists of some parents—after career, education, self-esteem and personal enjoyment. They are also being abused, but God views them as a godly heritage (Psalm 127:3) rather than an option.

At the same time, children no longer respect their parents. They considered their parents antiquated. They ignore their opinions and decisions, and some children even attack their parents in order to fulfill their own desires and wishes. In the midst of conflicting priorities between parents and children, Paul presents straightforward directives that form essential principles for the parent-child relationship.

The command to children in verse 1 is to *obey*—from a Greek word made up of two words that mean "under" and "hear." Children are exhorted to respond to the direction of their parents.

The phrase *in the Lord* means that the motivation for obeying is not the command of the parent—it is a call and command of the Lord for children obey their parents. The word *right* indicates that the kind of obedience described is faithfulness to the commands and service of the Lord.

"Honour thy father and mother; which is the first commandment with promise; that it may be well with thee, and thou mayest live long on the earth" (6:2, 3). These two verses extend the idea of what is "right" for children to do in relationship to parents. Doing the right thing begins with obedience and continues with honoring.

Honour comes from a Greek word *tima*, which means "to count something or someone as valuable." It is to revere and recognize the value of another person. In this case, the child is to take on an attitude of respect and appreciation for the parent and what the parent has done.

The concept of doing what is right as a child and honoring parents is climaxed with the promise of receiving that which is "well." *Well* comes from a word that emphasizes security and completeness. The concept extends to relationships and circumstances with others. Character development and proper perspectives about life are to be founded upon right parent-child relationships. These will yield the fruit of secure and wholesome relationships in general. On the contrary, conflict between children and parents will produce distortion in relationships.

The promise of longevity sets the tone of the "wellness" promised. The promise is an enduring one and is part of a life of faith. It is part of the Ten Commandments given to Moses in Exodus 20:12. The longevity God grants is not just a promise of more days on earth. The act of honoring parents is not just a principle, but an act of faith in relationship to God. The benefit of living long on the earth is the result of that faith relationship, not just the honor given to the parent.

Additional insight on bringing up children. Ephesians 6:4, "And, ye fathers, provoke not your children to wrath: but bring them up in the nurture and admonition of the Lord," highlights the relationship of fathers to children. It does not reduce the importance of the role of mother. The father may have been cited here because of a particular need on the part of the Corinthian church. Even though the mother is not mentioned, this admonition can apply to both parents. The items mentioned in verse 4 pertain to skills and functions that are important for both parents to practice.

There are four different parenting skills mentioned in this verse. The first is to not provoke a child to wrath. The Greek word for *provoke* comes from two Greek words— "bringing someone" and "alongside." The description is someone who is angry. It also means to create a situation or relationship in which anger is manifested. The anger depicted here is a deep-seated, damaging anger that distorts and tears down relationships. Parents are also admonished to avoid circumstances and dynamics that foster harmful anger and intimidation.

The second skill mentioned is to *bring them up*, to "nourish" them and "tenderly care for" them. This is a process of growth and development of children who are fed and nurtured with encouragement.

The third skill is to *nurture* a child. This word comes from a Greek concept that means to "train" children with skills that will help them grow and mature.

The fourth skill is to nurture the child with *admonition*, a word that is used to indicate times when reproofs and corrections are necessary. It indicates that parents should set and maintain boundaries for the benefit of the child.

All of these skills are to be done "of the Lord." The boundaries, sources of encouragement and attitudes developed between the parent and child must come from the Lord.

In both the child's relationship to the parent and the parent's relationship to the child, dependence upon the

Lord is vital. The obedience and honor given to the parent by the child comes from a faith relationship rooted in Christ. The skills parents develop to relate to the child come from depending on the Lord.

Church of God Historical Review

In the very first General Assembly of the Church of God, the topic emphasized most was the family. The entry in the *Minutes* is significant:

> Family Worship . . . we recommend and urge that the families of all the churches engage in this very sacred and important service, at least once a day, at the time most convenient to the household, and that parents should see that every child is taught as early as possible to reverence God and their parents by listening quietly by and attentively, to the reading of God's Word and get down on their knees during the prayer (*Minutes*, 1906, p. 16).

The importance of the family is not only a ministry for each home, but it is also part of the concern of the church, especially the leadership of the church. The devotion and development of the family in faith and practice was a major priority. The record of the first General Assembly continues:

> We recommend further that the Deacons and each church use their influence, and make special effort to encourage every family in the church to engage in this devotional exercise everyday, and further to ascertain the proper information and make a report of the number of families who have been induced to take up this service during the year, the number of families that make it a regular practice and those who do not, and carry such report to the yearly or General Assembly (*Minutes*, 1906, p. 16).

CHAPTER EIGHT

BEHAVIORAL TEMPERANCE

Behavioral temperance is the second discipleship value that evolves from the great commandment to love self and neighbor. No matter what a person may claim his or her spiritual, mental or emotional condition to be, behavior is the ultimate indicator of the person's true condition. Disciples of Christ are not free to act as they please. Christ's commands and teachings form a boundary that tempers our actions. We live within that boundary of temperance. The boundary is for the security, witness and true empowerment of the believer.

We will practice temperance in behavior and will abstain from activities and attitudes which are offensive to our fellowman or which lead to addiction or enslavement.

There are at least three practices that address the boundaries set for the Christian by Scripture: temperance of behavior, denying offensive behavior and avoiding practices that lead to addiction and enslavement. The principles and scriptures behind these practices are analyzed below.

Temperance

Temperance in lifestyle is the first boundary. Just as metal is tempered through a process of heating and cooling that makes it stronger, so the believer is tempered for the kingdom of God. God calls the believer to make adjustments that are often unpleasant, but the end result is that the believer is more effective in working for God. One of the cardinal Christian virtues is temperance or self-control (1 Corinthians 9:25; Titus 1:8; 2:2). It is listed as fruit of the Spirit (Galatians 5:23). We are admonished to practice moderation and balance in our behavior (Philippians 4:5). The Scripture indicates that it is within our prerogative to control our thinking (Philippians 4:8), our anger (Ephesians 4:26) and our communication (Ephesians 4:29; Colossians 3:8). To exercise self-discipline reflects the power of God in our life (1 Corinthians 9:27; 2 Peter 1:5-11).

Temperance and self-control. In 1 Corinthians 9, Paul explained his disciplined approach to life and ministry. Verses 25-27 were part of his summary. This word *temperance* comes from a Greek word that means "from self-training." It emphasizes repeating an activity in order to improve. It also emphasizes having the ability to develop that which is good, while removing the bad. To fulfill the goals and calling God has for us, we must master this important discipline.

Titus 1:8 and 2:2 give the following principles of temperance:

Concept	Definition
Hospitality	Willing to help strangers
Lover of good men	Devotion to the best in others
Sober	Abstinence from controlling things (literally: "clear-headed")
Just	Devotion to upright things
Holy	Devotion and spirituality
Temperate	Self-training and control
Grave	Moral respectability
Sound in faith	Vibrant, healthy faith
Sound in charity	Love that is living
Sound in patience	Actively exercising patience

Fruit of the Spirit. Temperance is one of the aspects of the fruit of the Spirit (Galatians 5:23, KJV). Individuals cannot achieve the self-control needed in life on their own. True, complete and lasting temperance that is acceptable before God is only possible through the work of the Spirit.

Moderation. Important principles of moderation are given in Philippians 4:5. *Moderation* comes from a Greek word that means "under authority or another standard." It refers to making decisions with a strong awareness of standards. A person of moderation is not presumptuous, but demonstrates humility and patience with an awareness of these higher standards. In this verse, the phrase "the Lord is at hand" indicates that the standard was the Lord himself.

Controlling our thinking. Philippians 4:8 calls for a certain kind of thinking. *Thinking* comes from a Greek term that emphasized formulation of thought and carrying out intentions. Believers must continually center their thoughts on the following encouragements from Philippians 4:

Concept	Definition
True	Abiding truth
Honest	Same as "grave" (Titus 2:2)
Just	Upright by God's standard
Pure	Undefiled
Lovely	Pleasing before God
Good report	Godly reputation
Virtue	Produces godly character
Praise	Glorifies God

Controlling anger. Anger is referred to in Ephesians 4:26 as emotion that is not monitored or is out of control (v. 27). This verse does not speak against the existence of emotions. Rather, it warned against opening a door of opportunity for Satan to work (v. 27).

Controlling communication. In these verses, *communication* refers to the way people related to one another. The believer was to relate in an "edifying" way. This term means "to build up others." The opposite is to habitually damage someone's reputation. Our speech is to be a ministry (v. 29) and not be "filthy," that is, ungodly and harmful to another person's spiritual condition (Colossians 3:8).

Self-discipline reflects the power of God (1 Corinthians 9:27; 2 Peter 1:5-11). These passages emphasize the responsibility we have for our own behavior. We are not forced into ungodly behaviors by circumstances, heredity or environment. These may contribute to sinfulness; however, sin is rooted in our choices. Paul said in 1 Corinthians 9:27 that even he would be a castaway from the faith if he did not exercise self-discipline. Peter taught that the believer must be "diligent to make your calling and election sure" (2 Peter 1:11). If this were not done, a person would fall from the faith.

In verses 5-11, Peter gave a number of concepts that reflect self-discipline and control in the Christian life:

Concept	Definition
Faith	Relationship of Christ within
Virtue	The energy of a Godly life
Knowledge	Learning from knowing Christ
Temperance	Same as 1 Corinthians 9:25
Patience	Ability to endure
Godliness	Life centered in God
Brotherly kindness	Loving tenderness for others
Charity	Love powered by God's love

Without temperance, it is difficult for a person to grow spiritually. Believers may have the very best resources such as books, tapes, and so forth, to help them grow, but if they do not have personal discipline to apply those resources, they are ineffective. A pastor must equip people in the area of temperance if they are to apply even the best resources to their lives.

Self-discipline and priorities. Effective development of behavioral temperance requires understanding of other areas that affect behavior. It takes an integrated approach to change behavior. As the believer emphasizes other vital areas that are related to behavior and temperance, behavioral temperance increases. The other areas of life that are related to behavioral temperance and enhance self-control include the following:

1. *Spiritual priorities.* Lasting change in behavior begins with a spiritual change. The power of the Holy Spirit changes a person's behavior. Walking in the Spirit (Galatians 5:12-26), being filled with the Spirit (Ephesians 5:1—6:9) and not grieving the Holy Spirit (Ephesians

4:15-32) are vital components that bring about significant behavioral change.

2. *Emotional behavior.* Emotions are the impulses that drive behavior. Behavior does not occur without motivation. Effective pastoral action will recognize the relationship between emotions and behavior. Those who are given emotional rewards for godly behavior will continue to carry out those behaviors. However, if negative emotions are attached to the behavior—no matter how right those behaviors are—they will be discouraged in doing them.

This is why Paul said to "rejoice in the Lord alway" (Philippians 4:1-13). His joy was based on the Lord, not his emotions. But his relationship did have an impact on his emotions. Godly emotions provide the fuel for lasting behavioral change.

3. *Thinking.* In the same passage about labor and behavioral perseverance, Paul emphasized the importance of godly thinking. The discipline needed for behavioral change is not only personal, it is also mental. Paul's emphasis on godly thinking provided direction for the Philippians' behavior (Philippians 4:1-13). In the same manner, encouraging individuals to fill their minds with the right material will lead them toward the right behavior.

The self-monitoring, that is, temperance, of the mind is critical for behavioral temperance. Without godly thinking, there will not be godly behavior. If a pastor wants to change a person's behavior, he must address the following elements:

- *A change in content.* The memory of the person must also be transformed, a process which occurs through self-discipline, casting down thoughts which are not of God (2 Corinthians 10:1-6) and preserving thoughts which are of God (Philippians 4:1-13).

- *Behavioral changes*. Without behavioral changes, religion remains simply an idea or emotion. When a life is truly changed by God, those changes will be evident in the person's behavior. This is why pastoral ministry should specify the behaviors that are part of godliness. If a pastor avoids providing behavioral goals for the congregation and for individual believers, their faith will remain weak and incomplete. True spirituality is more than feeling and ideas; it is changed behavior as well.

- *Modeling good behavior.* Those we admire and elevate are our behavioral models. The pastor can emphasize behavioral temperance by being aware that he is a model for others, whether he realizes it or not.

- *Practice right relationships*. Even though we develop self-discipline while we are alone, it must eventually be practiced in relationship with others. Pastoral guidance in behavior must include both personal and relational goals for growth in behavioral changes. The minister must encourage right relationships to ensure Christian community.

Behavior is important because it is a barometer of the condition of other areas. This is why pastoral ministry must stress good behavior and assist in completing the work done in the areas mentioned above. The work of the Lord in a person's spirit, soul, emotions and mind finds its completion in godly behavior.

Offensive Behavior

The believer must act in love and sensitivity toward others. Having a vacuum mentality—assuming that others are not affected by what we do—is unChristian. The avoidance of offensive behavior can be summarized in the following statement:

The Bible speaks clearly that we are to be sensitive to the needs and feelings of others as a demonstration of our love for them (Matthew 22:39; Romans 12:9-21; 13:10; Philippians 2:3-5). At times it is necessary for us to control our behavior so as not to bring offense to others (Romans 14:13-21; 1 Corinthians 8:9-13). As we know Christ after the Spirit, we are also to know others in the same manner so we will not judge them after their outward behavior alone (2 Corinthians 5:16). A respect and tolerance for differences in others should characterize our relationships (Romans 14:2, 3; 1 Corinthians 8:8; Ephesians 4:2; Colossians 3:13; 1 Timothy 4:1-5).

Sensitivity to others. The passages listed above show how to adjust your behavior to meet the needs of others.

In Romans 12:9-21 we find a list of attributes of love and behavior that are exhibited when we are sensitive to others:

Concept	Definition
Love without dissimulation	Unhypocritical love
Abhor evil	Be horrified about evil
Cleave to good	Be "glued" to the good
Kind affection	Family-like tenderness to others
Preferring others	Giving honor to others
Not slothful in business	Not laziness, but godly responsibility
Rejoice in hope	God-centered goals
Patient in tribulation	Ability to persevere with others
Continue in prayer	Prayerful about all things

Distribute to necessity	Willing to meet needs
Given to hospitality	Open to helping strangers
Bless	Place God's priorities above all
Rejoice/weep	Sensitive to other's condition
Same mind	Share goals with others regardless of social standing
Recompense no evil	Do not try to gain by evil means
Provide honesty	Open and true before others
Live peaceably	Guided by peaceful goals
Don't avenge self	Reliance upon God regarding the evil of others toward you

Not bringing offense to others. In Romans 14:13-21 and 1 Corinthians 8:9-13, Paul gave instructions about sensitivity toward others. The issue in these passages was eating meat in the ancient culture of Rome and Corinth that had been previously offered to idols by the government or Temple authorities. Eating the meat may not have violated a personal conviction of a believer; however, it would have violated Christian love if eating the meat would hurt or "destroy" (Romans 14:15) the faith of another believer.

Not judging. Second Corinthians 5:16 indicates that a Christian's perception is not to be guided by priorities of the flesh. Rather, God-centered, Christlike priorities must guide the perspective of the believer.

Respect and tolerance (Romans 14:2, 3; 1 Corinthians 8:8; Ephesians 4:2; Colossians 3:13; 1 Timothy 4:1-5). The message of these passages is that a Christ-centered perspective of others should create respect and tolerance for them. Even though a person may be different according to human standards, by the standards of Christ's love, mercy and grace, they were to be loved and cared for by the believer.

In Romans 14:2, 3 and 1 Corinthians 8:8 there was a call for equality and submissiveness to one another because of the love of Christ. In Ephesians 4:2 emphasis was further made on the character qualities of humility and longsuffering toward others because of the presence of Christ within the believer. In Colossians 3:13 a forgiving attitude toward others is emphasized because of the forgiveness toward the believer. First Timothy 4:1-5 emphasizes the importance of thanksgiving and dependence on God in loving others.

Addiction and Enslavement

Partaking of certain substances, engaging in particular habits and indulging in various activities can lead to the loss of self-control. While most of life can be enjoyed, certain pleasures can become addictive. The enjoyment is only for a season. The avoidance of addictive and enslaving practices is affirmed in the following statement:

> One of the primary benefits of our liberty in Christ is freedom from the domination of negative forces (John 8:32, 36; Romans 6:14; 8:2). We are counseled not to put ourselves again under bondage (Galatians 5:1). Therefore, a Christian must totally abstain from all alcoholic beverages and other habit-forming and mood-altering chemical substances and refrain from the use of tobacco in any form, marijuana and all other addictive substances, and further, must refrain from any activity (such as gambling or gluttony) which defiles the body as the temple of God or which dominates and enslaves the spirit that has been made free in Christ (Proverbs 20:1; 23:20-35; Isaiah 28:7; 1 Corinthians 3:17; 5:11; 6:10; 2 Corinthians 7:1; James 1:21).

Freedom from domination of negative forces (John 8:32, 36; Romans 6:14; 8:2). These passages describe the power of the forces of evil. They can control and dominate a life if a person gives over to them. In John 8:32-36 the Lord declared that a sinner becomes a "servant" of sin. The only means of release from this enslavement was Christ. In Romans 6:14 and 8:2 Paul stressed that sin can have "dominion" over a life. *Dominion* comes from a Greek word that means "to have control or mastery." The only release from this vice is through faith in Christ.

Not putting ourselves under bondage. Galatians 5:1 emphasizes the concept of bondage. Opposite of bondage is liberty through Christ. Bondage entangles and makes you unable to "stand fast" in Christ. When individuals give in to sinful behavior, they remove themselves from the security and steadfastness of Christ, become subject to the wills and vices of evil, and bound in their behavior, not free to be strong and firm in Christ.

Bondage is self-inflicted. No one is forced to sin. Continual acceptance of sin renders a person a servant to sin. This cycle can always be broken by the power of Christ. However, servants of sin continue to refuse Christ's work. There must be total abstinence from addictive substances and activities that defile the body or dominate and enslave the spirit (Proverbs 20:1; 23:20-35; Isaiah 28:7; 1 Corinthians 3:17; 5:11; 6:10; 2 Corinthians 7:1; James 1:21).

The inherent deception of alcohol (Proverbs 20:1; 23:20-35; Isaiah 28:7). The emphasis of these passages is twofold. First, abstain from the consumption of alcoholic beverages. Second, there is the potential for overindulgence and ruin. The verses are not merely speaking against overindulgence. The emphasis is on the harmful effects that are inherent in alcohol already. Overindulgence is not ignored. In fact, overindulgence of food (gluttony) is mentioned in Proverbs 23:20, 21. However, alcohol received further illustration because there is the potential of addiction in alcohol that is not present in food.

Effect on our relationship with God (1 Corinthians 3:17; 5:11; 6:10; 2 Corinthians 7:1; James 1:21). These passages teach that a person's relationship with God is negatively affected by alcohol. It is a violation of the holiness God intended for a person's physical body. The operation of the Spirit of God within a person is diminished and eventually removed by the use of alcohol. Spirituality and alcohol cannot coexist because alcohol is a violation of the pureness of God and contradicts the work of the Holy Spirit.

Additional Insights

In 2 Timothy 3:16, 17, Paul expresses concern about the models of behavior that individuals were following. He felt that the peril of the end times (v. 1) was that the behavior and example of others were leading people in the church astray (vv. 2-9). In response, Paul challenged Timothy to change his actions and become behaviorally temperant himself (vv. 10-15). The actual process of behavioral temperance and change that Paul taught is found in verses 16 and 17.

Inspiration, doctrine and spiritual temperance. The first element was spiritual. This has been mentioned earlier in this chapter. Paul's references to the inspiration of the Word and doctrine indicate the foundation of spiritual priorities. Timothy's life and behavior had to be rooted in this foundation.

Reproof and emotional temperance. Paul realized that if Timothy was to be an effective model, he had to encounter emotional reproof. *Reproof* comes from a Greek

word that means "to convict." It means changing someone's direction. This was a very emotional experience of
confrontation. The necessary adjustments begin in the
mind. With the mind clearly focused on what must be
changed, goals can be formulated. With a change in
thinking and an understanding of goals and priorities,
new behaviors can then be learned.

Instruction and behavioral temperance. As mentioned
earlier in this chapter, changing behavior itself is a process
of teaching and learning. This is why Paul stresses the
necessity of instruction. For the work of the Spirit within
the emotions and the mind to be complete, instruction in
behavior must take place.

Perfecting relational temperance. The last area Paul
emphasized is relationships. The word *perfect* comes from
a Greek concept that means "to fit into." The changes
wrought by the Word and the Spirit in emotions, mind and
behavior must be developed in the context of relationships. This is where the other changes are perfected and
applied.

Just as Paul ministered to Timothy about change and a
godly, temperant lifestyle, today's pastor must emphasize behavioral temperance. The temptation that draws
many away from the faith is ungodly models. Paul challenges Timothy to experience and teach the necessity to
be changed completely, in spirit, emotions, mind, behavior and relationships. This chapter has covered all these
areas because a change in behavioral temperance is only
possible when all of these areas are changed as well.

Striving for mastery in living. First Corinthians 9:25
calls for temperance in order to be able to master other
areas of life. "And every man that striveth for the mastery is temperate in all things. Now they do it to obtain a
corruptible crown; but we an incorruptible."

The word *temperate* comes from two Greek words, *en* and *kratos,* which mean "in control." The control is one of dominion and strength, exercising control over every facet of daily living.

The illustration in this verse depicts an athlete who controlled his lifestyle in order to perform better. In similar fashion, the believer must be controlled by the power of the Lord in order to glorify God. This serves as the foundation for further mastery in other areas of life.

Church of God Historical Review

From the very earliest General Assemblies, the Church of God has had a long-standing position advocating the importance of self-control and self-discipline. This section will review some of the decisions and notations recorded in the early minutes of the General Assembly that reflected this stand.

Tobacco was warned against in the very first General Assembly in 1906. In the first appearance of the Church of God Teachings in 1910, there were clear admonitions against using substances that were contrary to the virtues of self-control and temperance. Total abstinence from all liquor or strong drinks is supported by the following scriptures: Proverbs 20:1; 23:29-32; Isaiah 28:7, 1 Corinthians 5:11; 6:10, Galatians 5:21, 23. The church taught against the use of tobacco in any form, opium, morphine, and so forth (Isaiah 55:2, 1 Corinthians 10:31, 32; 2 Corinthians 7:1; Ephesians 5:3-8; James 1:21 (*Minutes,* 1912, p. 31).

In the first General Assembly, the sixth item discussed was the use of tobacco. The first five items were the judicial function of the Assembly, record keeping procedure, communion and feet washing, prayer meetings and evangelism. The Assembly gave personal discipline and the avoidance of tobacco a high priority along with the other items. The record regarding tobacco was as follows:

> A discourse on the "Use of Tobacco" was delivered by Evangelist M.S. Lemons and discussed by others. After due consideration this Assembly agrees to stand, with one accord, in opposition to its use. It is offensive to those who do not use it; weakens and impairs the mind and nervous system; is a near relative to drunkenness; bad influence and example to the young; useless expense, the money for which ought to be used to clothe the poor, spread the gospel or make the homes of our country more comfortable; and last we believe its use to be contrary to the teaching of the Scripture, and as Christ is our example we cannot believe that He would use it in any form or under any circumstances....We further recommend and advise that the deacons of each church make special effort to use their influence against its use, deal tenderly and lovingly with those in the Church who use it, but insist with an affectionate spirit, that its use be discontinued as much as possible. We, also, advise them to secure a report, at the close of each year, the number that have been induced to discontinue the habit and delivered from its desire for it, as to the number that still continue its use, and carry such report to the General Assembly" (pp. 14, 15).

This was a kind, compassionate and clear statement regarding the use of tobacco. It reflects the definite stance and conviction of the early Church of God founders. Also, within this text is the assumption that alcohol and drunkenness were contrary to godliness. The evils of tobacco are amplified and illustrated by comparing it to drunkenness. This statement can also be taken as a reflection of the church's early stance regarding the use of alcohol.

The record emphasizes the responsibility of the individual and the church. The church was to be clear about its stance but active in its care and compassion for those who were subjecting themselves to the influences of tobacco and alcohol.

In subsequent Assemblies, there were other issues discussed regarding tobacco. Adjustments were made regarding the position on tobacco. Issues included tobacco, church offices and membership. Even though it was addressed in the 1906 record, it continued to be a point of discussion. In 1908 statements and adjustments were made regarding this issue.

> The following questions were discussed and answers given. Does the use of tobacco disqualify a man for the office of deacon? Answer: Yes without a dissenting voice. . . . It was finally decided that those in the church who use tobacco should be dealt with kindly, fairly and squarely and given a little time for consideration and those who rigidly refuse to discontinue the use of tobacco in a reasonable length of time be disfellowshipped. . . . Among the scriptures found upon which to base this conclusion were the following: Isaiah 55:2; 2 Corinthians 7:1; Galatians 5:19, 21; Ephesians 5:3-7. (In addition, the assembly decided that the use of tobacco disqualifies a person for becoming a member of the Lord's church, *1908 General Assembly Minutes*, p. 33, 35).

The issue of tobacco and membership continued into the next General Assembly in 1909. In that Assembly, certain portions of the 1908 statement were deleted. This was the first item of business in the 1909 Assembly, perhaps highlighting the level of concern that the previous statement be adjusted. The deletions reflect care and compassion in ministry.

There were a few decisions made about other substances that were not addictive. In these the Assembly exercised wisdom with caution. In the January, 1913 General Assembly there was a notation and advisement about coffee.

> Remarks by the General Overseer. Q. Is it a sin to drink coffee, eat meat etc. and wear collars and ties? A. Some have gotten into erroneous ideas because they do not see the weightier things and the reason of this is for a lack of knowledge. It might be well to speak of coffee occasionally in private conversation regarding its stimulating effect as it gives some people the headache to do without it. I believe our folks would be better off without it, but we cannot bring it in the church as a doctrine. We should be careful about saying harsh, rasping things about it that would hurt the feelings of brothers and sisters. Pork may not be good for some people and we might all be better off if we did not use it, but if one wants to eat it and another does not there should be no fault-finding with each other about it. 'The kingdom of God is not meat and drink; but righteousness, and peace, and joy in the Holy Ghost' (January, 1913, pp. 69-70).

In the 1917 General Assembly a number of statements were made regarding substances other than alcohol. Many of these were relatively new products and substances for that day. Some of the chemical mixtures used for them contained drug derivatives that were suspected to be addictive.

These responses never became part of the actual Church of God Teachings or a test of membership in the church. These responses were either not printed in the succeeding Minutes or they were formally ruled out; e.g. vote on items to include in the Supplement in 1931 General Assembly, p. 38 and the vote to remove the statement on Coca Cola in 1935 General Assembly, p. 36.

The notations were made as part of the General Overseer's address when he spoke concerning the teachings of the church. Evidently, he received and answered a few questions at the time. The record of this event was as follows:

Question.—What about coca cola and other cold drinks? I hope none of our people are guilty of drinking such things, but if they are I hope they won't do it any more. I wonder what next. It looks like the devil has many traps set for us, but he is not going to get us all. Question.—What about chewing gum? This is not a test of membership, but our people should not use it. We will not give a person credentials to preach if they use the stuff. Question.—Is it wrong to drink coffee? Some drink it and some do not. But I notice that when coffee drinkers do not get their coffee they have the headache. This makes me think it may be wrong to use it. I do not hear of headaches when people do not get their milk or water. The Assembly has not made any rules about coffee, and it is not good to preach about it or even mention it much and thus probably hurt the feelings of some of our people who use it. We can discourage the use of it by being without it ourselves. Question. What about soda water? Some one asked me about that recently and I told them that they might use a little soda in some water at home and drink it if they wanted to, but they should never buy it and drink it at any of these public drink stands. [The following question was part of the action of the Assembly as a whole.] Q. What should be done with a bishop who sells cold drinks, such as soda water, and coca cola? Ans. He must not do it. He should quit it and get another job. The assembly has long since decided against such practice. Bishops, deacons, evangelists or members should not sell such things (*1917 General Assembly Minutes*, pp. 27-29, 43).

The decisions and discussions of the 1917 Assembly are more limiting than the notations of the 1913 Assembly. There is some comment regarding coffee that encourages love and understanding in dealing with the issue. This was the theme of the notations in 1913. However, in the majority of the 1917 notations, there is little tolerance and appeal to love and tenderness in its enforcement.

Another example of the Assemblies' advisements and wisdom about other substances is an entry in the 1930 General Assembly regarding "Coca Cola" and "bottled beverages" (1930 General Assembly Minutes, p. 21). The advisement was later repealed by vote of the 1935 General Assembly (1935 General Assembly, p. 36).

COCA COLA DISCOURAGED Whereas, there is a great deal of dissatisfaction among our ministers and laity concerning those that drink Coco Cola, we recommend that the use of Coco Cola and all other bottled drinks be very much discouraged to the extent that each one that indulges may understand that they are violating a general sentiment that it is very unbecoming" (1930 General Assembly, p. 21).

In the 1910 General Assembly a committee was commissioned to formulate examination questions for ministerial candidates (p. 46, 47). The report of the committee was first printed in the Church of God official paper then called, The Evening Light and Church of God Evangel. Their report included the first form of the Teachings of the Church of God. The Church of God Teachings were listed with the following items regarding tobacco and other substances:

Total abstinence from all liquor or strong drinks Proverbs 20:1; 23:29-32; Isaiah 28:7; 1 Corinthians 5:11; 6:10; Galatians 5:21, 23. Against the use of tobacco in any form, opium, morphine, etc.: Isaiah 55:2; 1 Corinthians 10:31—32; 2 Corinthians 7:1; Ephesians 5:3-8; James 1:21 (*The Evening Light and Church of God Evangel,* Vol. 1, No. 12, Aug. 15, 1910, p. 3).

In dealing with the difficulties of behavior and temperance, the early General Assembly records indicated a concern and sensitivity for others. The notations already cited regarding tobacco and other practices indicated a compassionate, pastoral approach to these areas. Indicative of this sensitivity was a sermon delivered by R.G. Spurling on the primacy of love. He compared the law of love to an important link in a railroad track, making the railway complete. He said, "One of these golden rails represents the law, 'Thou shalt love the Lord thy God with all thy heart.' and the other, 'Thou shalt love thy neighbor as thy self'" (*January, 1913 General Assembly Minutes*, p. 40).

Another example of this priority on love and pastoral sensitivity was an appeal to avoid divisions. General Overseer A.J. Tomlinson made the following statement in the same General Assembly:

In the time of Nehemiah they had to put away their strange wives. It is time for us to put away our strange ideas and opinions and get God's mind. When Jesus stood before Pilate His judgment was taken away in His humiliation and He was dumb. At times it would be better for us not to open our mouths. What is the use to cavil over small matters? The ministers who engage in criticizing and picking flaws with one another in private conversation, make me think they have quit the fight against the one great enemy. What is the use to cavil over small matters of small importance such as coffee, meats etc.? Let us deal with the weightier things! Let us notice the government of Jesus! Paul did not depend on visions and interpretations, but on the Word of God. It is God's plan for the younger to submit to the Elder, but one is not an Elder who is not humble and submissive. The little streams and divisions must all be covered up with the flood tide of greater things. We must stand together. No division over coffee, meats etc. Look at the more important things that will save souls. Judge not in meats and drinks. I have no time to bother with such little things. God knows my heart is in this thing. Remember that in F.J. Lee's address he spoke about Paul sending men likeminded with himself who were to teach the things that he taught and nothing more. 'My people are destroyed for lack of knowledge' is true today. If you want to show your ignorance just begin to cavil about things. There are a kind of stiff-necked people today like those in the time of Moses where God said, Let me alone that I may destroy them for they are a stiff necked people, but Moses fell on his face before God instead of caviling with them, and staid there until God granted his request. A set of strong men are needed today who will fall on their faces before God rather than strive and cavil over questions of no value. Let us get one heart and one soul. . . . (*January, 1913 General Assembly*, pp. 58-59).

CHAPTER NINE

REPRESENTING CHRIST IN THE WORLD

Jesus pronounced the purpose of the disciples' love—
"A new commandment I give unto you, That ye love
one another; as I have loved you, that ye also love
one another. By this shall all men know that ye are my
disciples, if ye have love one to another" (John 13:34,
35).

The previous sections have looked at the two greatest commandments, loving God and loving self and
others. Discipleship values that grew out of both of
those two commands have been presented. The love
and subsequent values of the two greatest commandments would be incomplete without taking the witness
of God's love to the world. Jesus' words expressed
that by our love the world would know Him.

What values grow out of our love and witness to the
world? At least two can be emphasized, modest
appearance and social obligation. Modest appearance
emphasizes our personal witness to the world. Social
obligation emphasizes our community witness to the

world. Chapter 10 will review the value and practices of modest appearance. Chapter 11 will present the value and practices of social obligation. Before moving on to those values, this chapter will look further at the nature of the believer's witness and love to the world.

The Power of Personal Conduct

The personal conduct and ethics of a believer make a strong statement of faith to others. The local congregation and the community observe the conduct of the believer every day. Even more important is the personal conduct a believer displays before the family. It is important to look at the theological reasons and motivations for the believer's personal conduct and its resulting impact.

God has continually been involved in the world of His creation. He is the Creator and sustainer of this world (Isaiah 40). God did not merely create the world and then leave it to run by itself. In turn, the world reflects the involvement of the Creator. We and all God's creation were created to give glory and honor to Him (Genesis 1; 2; Romans 1).

The glory and honor due Him is tangible and real. The world and all of its substance are representative of His acts and glory. This includes the personal conduct of the believer.

The Influence of the Believer

Because the Word of God is written on the hearts of believers (2 Corinthians 3:3), the world observes the Word in the life of the Christian (v. 2). The writing is through the Holy Spirit (v. 6), and the magnitude of what is written is greater than the stones written on Mount Sinai (vv. 7-18). The writing on the hearts and lives of believers shine forth into the darkness of the world (4:6). The persecution and tribulations of the world cannot dim the message of the believer (vv. 7, 18). The new creation of Christ within the life of the believer is for the purpose of making the Christian an ambassador and representative of Christ to a disbelieving world (5:20).

Concern for All

Paul writes in Romans 1:14, "I am a debtor both to the Greeks, and to the Barbarians; both to the wise, and to the unwise." The love and concern of the believer is not limited to the *wise*. This word is descriptive of someone who has a certain level of awareness and sophistication. The word used in this verse comes from the Greek word *sophos*. It is the word from which we derive the word *sophisticated*, indicating someone who is "clever, informed and experienced." The word *Greek* refers to the fact that the Greeks possessed this quality because they were the most advanced and sophisticated culture at that time.

By comparison, *unwise* and *Barbarian* referred to those in society who did not possess the refinement and sophistication of that day. *Unwise* simply means those who did not possess nor practice the social and intellectual abilities of the "wise." *Barbarian* also referred to those who did not speak the same language and appeared awkward in society.

The love and concern of the believer should extend to the most sophisticated in today's society, as well as those who are not at ease in today's culture. It is impossible to be faithful to God's command to love others when preferential treatment is given to the "wise" of today's world and the "unwise" are shunned or ignored.

Restoring love that endures. Galatians 6:9, 10 instructs: "And let us not be weary in well doing: for in due season we shall reap, if we faint not. As we have therefore opportunity, let us do good unto all men, especially unto them who are of the household of faith."

In these verses Paul emphasizes the need for love that endures and extends to all persons. The person who is demonstrating love to others should not become weary because God will reward this kind of faithfulness.

This principle is important in light of the many temptations to become "weary in well doing." *Weary* does not mean mere physical exhaustion—it indicates becoming "fainthearted" or "lacking in courage to accomplish something." There are many things that test the love of believers for others. Paul exhorted the Galatians to not become cowards in the face of temptation.

The theme of Romans 6 is one of restoration and edification. Given this context, temptation to grow weary in love and well doing may have been in this same area. There may be temptations to fall into ridicule when restoring a fallen brother. Or the temptations may be personal doubts about the power of God to restore the fallen. The believer is to be encouraged that in due time, within God's providence, the rewards of enduring love will come.

Paul's conclusion in verse 10 is a summary for the work of enduring love and restoration. He says that the enduring love of believers should aim at restoring and reaching out to as many people as possible. This is the mission of love Christ has given the church to reach a lost and dying world.

At the same time, Paul places a priority on the household of faith. The precedent for this principle can be traced to the teachings of Jesus discussed in another lesson. In

John 13:34, 35, Jesus declared that the love of Christians for one another would be a testimony to the world. When Christians do good toward one another, they bear witness of the power of God's love.

Demonstrating Love as a Witness to Others

Owe no man any thing, but to love one another: for he that loveth another hath fulfilled the law. For this, Thou shalt not commit adultery, Thou shalt not kill, Thou shalt not steal, Thou shalt not bear false witness, Thou shalt not covet; and if there be any other commandment, it is briefly comprehended in this saying, namely, Thou shalt love thy neighbour as thyself (Romans 13:8, 9).

In this passage, Paul specifies one of the most important of Christian obligations—the obligation to love others. God works through us by calling us to minister to our neighbors. In the context of this chapter, this includes government officials (13:1-8).

The admonition, "owe no man any thing," must be connected to the latter part of the statement, "but to love one another." In this context, when you fail to love others, you are indebted to them. If the Christian fails to respond in this manner, the obligation remains until love is shown.

The reference to the law in the latter portion of verse 8 marks the overall significance of this indebtedness of love. All that the believer does in response to his neighbor, including reactions to authorities, comes under his obligation to respond in love.

In verse 9, Paul expanded the idea that love is the fulfilling of the law. He listed a number of the basic commandments. He then said that all the commandments come under the guideline and motivation of love.

Paul quoted the principle of love for your neighbor in the latter portion of verse 9. Jesus also quoted this principle in Matthew 22:39. They were taken from the section of the Law discussed earlier in Leviticus 19:18. This is the summary principle of relationships with others, even government authorities. It is the foundation for Paul's concept of relationships, Jesus' teaching about the witness of the church and principles in the Law about relationships.

Product of love. Romans 13:10 states: "Love worketh no ill to his neighbour: therefore love is the fulfilling of the law." This verse indicates the result of loving our neighbor—love "worketh no ill." Love for others produces the fulfillment of God's law in an individual's life.

The power of this concept is the context in which Paul presents it—government persecution and the demands of civil authorities. The early church was under oppression by governmental authorities. Paul exhorted them that their response must be an act of love for their neighbor.

The believer's actions will have an influence on fellow citizens. Paul labeled acts of resistance and rebellion as acts of evil (Romans 13:1-8). When believers fail to submit properly to God's sovereign action through rulers and authorities, they fail to love their neighbors.

It must be carefully noted that Paul was not endorsing evil rulers or the evil actions of neighbors. Neither was he advocating doing things contrary to the teachings of Christ because of a ruler's demands. Evil is never to be endorsed. Paul is emphasizing the Christian's basic obligation to recognize and cooperate with the sovereignty of God by always acting out of love for others.

The end product of such love will be the fulfillment of God's will on the earth. The greatest power on earth is the love of God. His sovereign action on nations and

authorities of the earth will bring them to eventual submission to Christ as Lord (Philippians 2:10). In the
mean-time, the Christian participates in this process rep-
resenting God in this world, by acting out of love for
God and others.

CHAPTER TEN

MODEST APPEARANCE

The first discipleship value that grows out of our love and witness to others is modest appearance. The word *modesty* comes from the Greek word *kosmos,* from which the modern word *cosmetic* comes. The word essentially means "order" or "arrangement." The implication of the word is an orderly presentation or goal and direction. The opposite is chaos and distortion. Modest living and dress reflects the goals and orderliness of a life patterned after godly principles.

The following statement affirms the Christian value of a modest appearance:

We will demonstrate the Scriptural principle of modesty by appearing and dressing in a manner that will enhance our Christian testimony and will avoid pride, elaborateness or sensuality.

The Scriptural principle of modesty along with a number of related scriptures are analyzed in this chapter.

Modesty

According to the Biblical idea, modesty is an inner spiritual grace that recoils from anything unseemly and impure, is chaste in thought and conduct, and is free of crudeness and indecency in dress and behavior (Ephesians 4:25, 29, 31; 5:1-8; 1 Timothy 2:9, 10). Therefore, modesty includes our appearance, dress, speech and conduct and can be applied to all situations. The essential issue is, does our style of life please or displease God?

Modesty and truth. Ephesians 4:25 discusses the concept of truth as it relates to a modest and orderly life. Paul admonishes the believer to be truthful in relationships with one another in the body of Christ. They are members of each other, indicating that they need one another and can function only if they dwelt in harmony and truth. The opposite of this concept is chaos and a lack of genuineness in relationships.

Modesty and edifying communication. Another important concept for modesty and godly goals for living is edifying communication (v. 29). In this verse Paul says that we need to minister to one another. Speech is a primary method of ministry to encourage, comfort and edify others.

Modesty and bitterness. Bitterness demonstrates a lack of direction from the Lord. Sadly, a person can become motivated by wrath, anger, clamor and evil speaking. These do not reflect modesty or godly character—they are self-centered and destructive. Immodest speech is marked by the qualities listed in Ephesians 4:31.

Adornment and modest apparel. In 1 Timothy 2:9, Paul gives specific instruction about dress for women that can be applied to men as well. Paul said their apparel should be modest and worn with "shamefacedness" and "sobriety." *Shamefacedness* comes from a Greek word that means "to hold back shame and dishonor"—dressing in a way that avoided dishonor, shame and immorality. Our dress must not encourage immorality or temptation.

Sobriety comes from a Greek word that means "self-control and discipline." Our dress is to reflect a lifestyle that has overcome lusts and temptations. In other words, we are to demonstrate spiritual victory and moral temperament through our dress.

Paul teaches the reader to avoid clothing that fails to demonstrate honor and self-control. Whatever the current fashions may be, believers' apparel should always reflect moral control and spiritual victory.

Appearance and Dress

The principles of proper appearance and dress are captured in the following statement:

> *Our life, character and self-image are reflected by our apparel and mode of dress. The admonition of Scripture, "Be not conformed to this world," reminds us that our manner of dress must be modest and decent (Romans 12:2; 1 Thessalonians 5:22, 23). It is not displeasing to God for us to dress well and be well-groomed. However, above all we must seek spiritual beauty, which does not come from outward adornment with jewelry, expensive clothes or cosmetics, but from good works, chaste conversation, and a meek and quiet spirit (Philippians 4:8; 1 Peter 3:3-5).*

Modest and decent dress (Romans 12:2; 1 Thessalonians 5:22, 23). The criteria by which someone dresses should be the principles listed in Romans 12:2—"that good, and acceptable, and perfect, will of God." Dress is only one area of our lives that reflects spiritual renewal or conformity to the world. Nevertheless, our dress does reveal the presence or absence of spiritual renewal.

Every individual follows some standard for dress. The standard may be set by one of the following influences:

- Principles of character

- Fashion worn by someone they admire

- Clothes that are simple and comfortable

Seeking the particular kind of apparel to wear should be a matter of prayer and devotion.

Appearance of evil (1 Thessalonians 5:22, 23). *Appearance* comes from a Greek word meaning "that which is visible" or "outward form." These verses emphasize the fact that the outward appearance is important. Ideas and inward characteristics are important, but they are incomplete without consideration of outward appearances. The idea or principle behind something is revealed by its appearance. The admonition by Paul in verse 22 is not just about the vague idea or abstraction of evil; it is about the *appearance* of evil, which can include dress.

Spiritual beauty. In Philippians 4:8 and 1 Peter 3:3-5, we see a number of characteristics to guide the Christian's thinking. These are important because they affect the outward behavior and appearance of the believer. This is why Paul summarized the list by saying that as the believers had "seen" him do these things inwardly and outwardly, they were to follow him (4:9).

Inward adornment. The context of 1 Peter 3:3-5 shows the importance of appearance matching and confirming a wife's testimony. These principles can be applied to both men and women. The conduct and appearance of believers should be enough to testify that their life is centered on the Word.

Verses 1 and 2 emphasize the character qualities of submission and godly fear that mark a person's dress. The opposite would be pride, rebellion and self-centeredness. Adornment should reflect godly character qualities. A primary way to determine the character qualities behind apparel is to notice the kinds of people who wear certain kinds of clothing. Clothing, especially in contemporary society, is used to make a statement about a person's character, lifestyle or morality.

In verse 3 Paul identified certain aspects of outward adornment that did not demonstrate the character qualities of submission and godly fear. These particular kinds of clothing and styles change from generation to generation and from culture to culture. However, if most of the people who dress in a certain manner are known for ungodly character qualities, should the believer be identified with those people and the qualities they represent?

Verses 4 and 5 describe the necessity of being guided by inner, godly qualities in dress. These qualities included:

Concept	Definition
Not corruptible	Focus on godly, eternal things
Meek	Willing to be submissive
Quiet	Not self-centered

In verse 4, Paul emphasized the necessity of pleasing God by our dress. The believer must come to God in prayer and find a sincere satisfaction that God is being honored and pleased by what is worn.

In verse 5, Paul mentioned the importance of examples and models of dress. Paul mentioned the example of the inner spirit of holy women in the past. He was not elevating their particular style of dress as much as their godly motivation. Their holiness and submissive spirit, especially in relationship to the home, were important examples to follow.

Today dress is often designed to allure individuals away from faithfulness to the home and spouse. Paul advocated that dress represent the priority we place on godly morality, the Christian home and family.

Pride, Elaborateness, Sensuality

The final practice that supports the value of modest appearance is the avoidance of pride, elaborateness and sensuality in appearance. The following statement confirms this avoidance:

> *As godly people we are to abstain from all lusts of the flesh and avoid dressing in a manner that encourages immoral thoughts, attitudes and lifestyles (Galatians 5:13-21; 1 Peter 2:11; 2 Peter 1:4). Our beauty does not depend on elaborate, showy dress; extravagant, costly attire; or on the use of jewelry or cosmetics but on our relationship with Christ. External adornment, whether clothing or jewelry, as an outward display of personal worth, is contrary to a spiritual attitude (James 2:1-4).*

Lusts of the flesh and dress. Dress, as mentioned in the previous section, is more than a personal issue. Galatians 5:13-21; 1 Peter 2:11; and 2 Peter 1:4 emphasize that victory and liberty are not the only basis for Christian living. Love and sensitivity for others are important factors to consider when making decisions about dress. The believer's appearance should not weaken the faith of another person.

Walking in the Spirit (Galatians 5:16-18). In order to avoid the temptations of dressing in a way that reflects compromise with worldly priorities or tempts others, a believer needs the power of the Spirit. The Spirit can guide us to the proper role models for character and dress. The Spirit can give inner motivation and guide decisions about dress. And, the Spirit can help develop goals of modesty that reflect order and godliness in appearance.

Works of lust and the flesh (vv. 19-21). These verses reflect the kind of characteristics that can become the goals of dress. Adulterous temptations, idolatry of individuals, conflicts in the spirit realm and angry strife are all communicated by forms of dress today. Individuals wear slogans on their apparel or design their clothes in certain styles that communicate a particular message. Christians need to be aware of the kind of message they are communicating with the clothing they wear.

The decision about dress is a faith decision. Clothing that does not reflect godly order or goals becomes an instrument the enemy can use to war against the strength of the believer. In 2 Peter 1:4 and 2:11 Peter identifies the struggle that is taking place for the soul and admonishes the believer to abstain from things that may cause him to weaken in this struggle. The decisions a Christian makes about apparel should reflect the preeminence of Christ rather than spiritual compromise.

Outward display of personal worth (James 2:1-4). Outward adornment should ultimately be a reflection of the Lord. In this passage, James questioned the readers about basing their worth on dress rather than a relationship with the Lord. Decisions about appearance are important not because of what they say about us, but what they say about the presence of the Lord within us.

Additional insights on the devotion of the Christian and outward apparel. Dress and adornment is part of the extension of our faith and devotion to the Lord. Our faith is more than what we wear, but what we wear is part of the manifestation of our faith. Specifying devotional methods as a way to develop godly dress should also be emphasized. We must develop pastoral approaches that do not merely emphasize outward appearance and adornment alone, but also stress inner spirituality.

Establishing the character of Christ within is the foundation for maintaining a godly appearance in apparel and dress. The attributes of love, devotion, holiness, modesty and others are important to develop. Apparel is not important in itself, but the manner in which it reflects certain character qualities is very important. What a person wears, to some significant degree, reflects a certain standard of morality. That standard is developed first and then the manner of dress follows.

There is a wide variety of adornments that can be worn to reflect the same qualities. The cultural circumstances and the meanings given to certain styles may change. What does not change is the importance of the character qualities being developed. If standards of adornment are based on interpretations of fashion or cultural norms alone, the standards will not last. What must last is the ability to develop godly character and then communicate those qualities in our dress.

The choice about adornment is not merely a decision of the individual. As with other aspects of the Christian life such as behavior, friendships and thoughts, the power to make godly choices comes from Christ and the Holy Spirit. Believers do not walk after the flesh, but after the Spirit. This principle applies in the area of dress as well. The believer's task with apparel is not how right clothes can be chosen as much as how the proper faith can be developed from which to make those choices.

The importance of appearance must not be overridden by the importance of character. The two areas compliment one another. The danger is to either eliminate appearance or emphasize appearance before character. The pastor must strongly emphasize Christ-like character as the foundation for appearance.

The greater threat is to totally ignore matters of dress. If outward appearance is continually ignored, the spirituality of the individual will be affected. Spiritual development bears fruit that can be seen in behavior, speech and dress. Eventually, dress has to be included in the spiritual growth of a person.

Outward adornment may reflect conflicting values. Priorities of dress will be in conflict with what may be developing in that person's spiritual life. For example, if the Lord is developing greater love and submission in the person, wearing clothes that represent rebellion and lust will weaken faith. If a person is having difficulty deciding what to wear as a believer, the place to begin is not the clothing but with the heart. Regular times of devotion, Scripture reading and attendance in church should be emphasized. Maintaining a spiritual journal, receiving godly counsel from the pastor and fasting should be stressed. Becoming strong in the faith is preparatory to decisions about outer adornment.

If difficulty in the area of modest appearance continues, individuals may need spiritual guidance and assistance from someone over them in the Lord. The person still makes the decisions about dress, but this process would reinforce the quality of submission. This is one of the most important character qualities stressed in Scripture and must be applied to both men and women (Ephesians 5:21).

Provide alternative role models for dress. An effective tool is to point out Christian individuals who are venerable and worthy of admiration. These persons become role models in character, as well as dress. As mentioned earlier, the kind of dress a person adopts reflects not only styles, but also role models. This was the principle Peter emphasized in 2 Peter 3:3. Negative role models and attitudes to avoid are also stressed by in James 2:1-4.

Choices about clothing are never isolated from the lifestyle of a person. The positive and negative aspects of clothing can be effectively illustrated when behavior and other lifestyle considerations are made.

These considerations include whether Christian or non-Christian behaviors are identified with certain styles of clothing. Is violence and crime associated with a particular style? Does rebellion and deceit mark particular forms of dress? The associations and behaviors labeled with styles may change. This is all the more reason why a person must ask about associations and characteristics attached with certain styles of clothing.

Church of God Historical Review

This section will review various statements and decisions in the very earliest General Assembly Minutes that relate to the area of modest appearance. There were no entries relating to modest appearance during the first seven General Assemblies. The first entries came in the January, 1913 General Assembly. The early statements centered on inner character and outward adornment, that is, pride and costly articles of clothing. Gradually, the emphasis moved to the theme of modesty. This continued as a major theme in the area of outward adornment.

From it's earliest General Assemblies, the Church of God endeavored to exercise moderation in matters of dress and personal practice. Harsh and condemning attitudes and character qualities were discouraged in such matters. The following excerpts from the January, 1913

General Assembly illustrate this point. Certain questions were asked about personal morality and the answers of the Assembly are recorded.

Q. Can we afford to adorn our bodies with gold or pearls or costly array? (See 1 Timothy 2:9, 1 Peter 3:3)....A. Unnecessary jewelry, such as finger rings, bracelets, ear-bobs, lockets, and other kinds for mere adornment should not be worn. Gold teeth, gold rimmed spectacles, watch cases and things specially useful are left for the individual to decide...., (January 1913, pp. 69).

That Assembly admonished the members that pride was a much greater sin than how a person dressed. Under particular discussion was the wearing of neckties (*Minutes,* January 1913, p. 70).

The first reference to outward adornment in a General Assembly occurred in the January, 1913 General Assembly when J.W. Buckalew mentioned it as part of a sermon entitled, "A Mourning for Pastors." It set a theme for further discussion and decisions on the topic later during the same Assembly. The mention in the sermon was as follows:

I went to a camp meeting and found a lot of sickly sheep and lambs caused by pride. The Lord laid it on my heart to preach against pride. Next day the precious girls came back with another story or two on their dresses and had laid aside their jewelry and about fifty of them fell into the altar and confessed their pride and the Lord wonderfully healed their backslidings. Preach the Word and have no respect of persons. Let the Gospel cut its way if it does hurt and your will have a lot of fat sheep ready for market (January, 1913, p. 65).

In the same General Assembly the general overseer also discussed modest apparel when he was asked a variety of questions:

Q. Is it a sin to drink coffee, eat meat etc. and wear collars and ties? A. Some have gotten into erroneous ideas because they do not see the weightier things and the reason of this is for a lack of knowledge....As to collars and ties, it is easy to get under bondage about such things. When the tabernacle and the temple were being constructed things were made for glory and beauty. It is good for people to appear neat in dress, and in many places you would have no influence with the people for good if you did not wear a collar and perhaps a tie. People sometimes become as proud in going slouchy as others in their vain dress. Paul as far as custom was concerned, became all things to all men that he might win some. Wear your collars, and ties if you want to, or if you do not want to wear a tie let the man alone that does. Such things are too trivial to mention when we have so much more important things for consideration (January, 1913, pp. 69-70).

The emphasis of these statements was on the development of godly character. Modest apparel was to reflect Christian character. The Assembly determined that outward appearance was to avoid pride, being too costly and an unnecessary part of the Christian life. The weightier things of Christlikeness were to be developed.

The tone of the language in the January, 1913 General Assembly was very pastoral when addressing the problem of how the Pentecostal believers were to dress. Modesty was certainly the more important criteria, a criterion of the heart. Pastoral compassion is very important in this process. The admonitions for mercy and not harshness are especially true of the individual shepherding a local congregation. So much of the compassion toward issues of modesty begin or can end with the example of the pastor.

The topic of outward appearance did not receive further attention until the 1917 General Assembly. In that Assembly there was a small, preliminary statement about apparel in the question and answer portion of the Assembly. The statement was, "We do not want our members to go to shows or wear superfluous gold" (1917 General Assembly, p. 28).

In the latter portion of the *Minutes* in a section called, "Instructions and Advices," the following notation was made, emphasizing the theme of moderation. The notation read,

> Your dress should be with moderation, neat and clean, but not for show. You should never wear gold for ornament or decoration. Finger rings, bracelets, earrings, necklaces, lockets and large show pins are not becoming for a saint of God....Abstain from the very appearance of evil (1917 *General Assembly Minutes*, p. 48).

Statements regarding the theme of modesty in dress continued to be printed in the early minutes. The following are three examples, 1929, 1933 and 1940.

> With reference to immodest apparel, we present the following resolution: After considering the question of immodest apparel among our people, we, as the board of counselors, desire to express our deep grief over the fact that many of our sisters in the Church of God are being overcome by the temptation to conform to the immodest dress of our day, and we recommend that the Assembly adopt this resolution, asking our sisters to prayerfully consider this matter and make an effort to improve these conditions by conforming to the apparel of modesty as revealed in the Scriptures. See Romans 12:1-2; 1 Timothy 2:9-16; Titus 2:3-5; James 4:4; 1 Peter 3:1-6; 1 John 2:15-17 (1929 *General Assembly Minutes*, p. 23).

At various times, specific styles of clothing were addressed at the assemblies of the 1920's and 1930's. These were not usually maintained as part of the minutes from year to year. They were usually in the context of suggestions rather than teachings. The following are examples of some of these statements and suggestions:

That the bobbing of hair of our members be discontinued but that mercy be shown those who already have their hair bobbed; but if after sufficient warning they disregard the advice given they should be dealt with in the Church of God (1925 *General Assembly Minutes*, p. 38).

Is age to be considered as to our members having bobbed hair? If they are mature enough to become members of the church they should be required to conform to its ruling and teaching on this matter (1927 *General Assembly Minutes*, p. 31).

An item was added to the Teachings in 1914 related to outward adornment. It was as follows, "26. Against members wearing gold for ornament or decoration, such as finger rings, bracelets, earrings, lockets, etc.—Isaiah 55:2; 1 Peter 3:3" (1914 General Assembly, p. 47).

There was an addition to article 26 in 1936 which read, ". . . except wedding rings in foreign countries where social laws or customs governing society require it" (1936 *General Assembly Minutes,* pp. 128-9). The addition was later deleted in 1938 (1938 *General Assembly Minutes*, pp. 97-8).

CHAPTER ELEVEN

SOCIAL OBLIGATION

The second discipleship value that grows out of our love and witness to others is social obligation. Loving others is not just for the church—it is for the world. Christ was in the world so much, loving and ministering to people, that He drew stiff criticism (Matthew 11:19; Luke 7:34). The scoffers thought He was too friendly with the sinners. In fact, Christ took the risk of reaching out to those in the world. He did not compromise godliness in order to take God to the ungodly. Christianity does not have to change in order to change the world. What does have to happen is a mobilization of love within the body of Christ to move beyond the church doors.

Christianity was never intended to be an exclusive club. A group that sits on the sidelines watching tragedies take place in the world and celebrating the fact that the world does not affect them is not accepting their social obligation to the world. On the contrary, the church owes a debt to Christ who came to them while they were away from the Father. The discipleship value that identifies the obligation to minister in society can be stated as follows:

It should be our objective to fulfill our obligations to society by being good citizens, by correcting social injustices, and by protecting the sanctity of life.

Discipleship values of social obligation include being good citizens, correcting social injustices, protecting the sanctity of life and caring for the earth and its resources. These practices, along with a number of supportive Scriptures are analyzed in the remainder of this chapter.

Being Good Citizens

The first practice that reflects the value of social obligation is being good citizens, affirmed in the following statement:

As Christians we are members of the kingdom of God as well as a social order of this world. Obedience to God requires us to act in a responsible manner as citizens of our country (Mark 12:13-17; Romans 13:1-7; 1 Peter 2:13-17). Therefore, we should support civil law and order; hold our leaders in respect and pray for them; participate in school, community and governmental activities; exercise our voting rights; and speak out on clear-cut moral issues. God's law is supreme, but we are to obey the laws of our country insofar as they are not in conflict with obedience to God (Acts 5:29). When it becomes necessary to disagree with practices and requirements of government, we should do so out of a concern for the promotion of righteousness and not out of delight in discord and controversy.

Responsible citizenship. We must clarify our obligations to the government and carry them out (Mark

12:13-17). God must be in ultimate control of what occurs (Romans 13:1-7). As a result, the believer is to be faithful to the Lord through responsible submission as a citizen.

Citizenship is never segregated from faith in these passages. The basis of carrying out our responsibility as a citizen is faith in God. God placed governments in His ultimate plan. Christians should not be remove from interaction with the government. Rather, they should seek direction from the Lord about ways to fulfill Christian faithfulness through responsible citizenship.

Romans 13:1-7 emphasizes several critical points regarding social obligation. Verse 1 stresses that governments are ultimately "subject" to or under the authority of God. God was the original and foremost source that "ordained" or set them in the order in which they are (i.e., power, control, influence, etc.).

Verse 2 reminds the believer that interaction and response to government is ultimately a response to God. Verse 3 is a reminder that the standards of godly character are guidelines for action, regardless of the condition of those in power. In verse 4, the reason for godly character as guidelines is because governments and rulers are instruments of God, carrying out His ultimate plan for the earth. Verses 5-7 emphasize the necessity to be faithful in governmental stewardship because it is a reflection of godly stewardship.

Obey laws that do not conflict with obedience to God (Acts 5:29). In the context of this verse, the church was being persecuted for spreading the gospel. They continued to preach the gospel because God called them to evangelize the world. Their response to the government was their prayerful appeal to the Lord that He empower and enable them to be obedient in spreading His Word, despite the opposition of the government.

Correcting Social Injustices

The second practice in fulfilling the discipleship value of social obligation is to correct injustice. The following statement affirms the practice of correcting injustices:

Love for others and the recognition of the equal worth of all people in the sight of God (Acts 10:34; 17:26) should compel us to take steps to improve the situation of those who are underprivileged, neglected, hungry, homeless and victimized by prejudice, persecution and oppression (Matthew 22:39; Romans 13:8-10; 1 John 3:17). In all of our dealings, we must be sensitive to human needs (Luke 10:30-37; James 1:17) and guard against racial and economic discrimination. Every person should have freedom to worship and participate in the life of the church regardless of race, color, sex, social class or nationality.

Recognition of equal worth. In Acts 10:34 Peter began his sermon in Cornelius' house by declaring God is no respecter of persons. Peter had a vision in which God emphasized this principle (Acts 10:9-18). The same principle is in the Old Testament law in Deuteronomy 10:17. That portion of the law stresses God's action among those in need:

For the Lord your God is God of gods, and Lord of lords, a great God, a mighty, and a terrible, which regardeth not persons, nor taketh reward: He doth execute the judgment of the fatherless and widow, and loveth the stranger, in giving him food and raiment. Love ye therefore the stranger: for ye were strangers in the land of Egypt (Deuteronomy 10:17-19).

In Acts 17:26 we find another portion of the Old Testament law—Numbers 16:22—as well as a portion of Isaiah 42:5. The emphasis is on God's action to all the nations. The purpose of His action is given in verse 27, "That they should seek the Lord, if haply they might feel after him, and find him, though he be not far from every one of us."

God's ultimate purpose in the care of the needy was that they might seek Him as Lord. The same purpose applies today. God is the center of the social obligation of the believer. Though the needs of individuals are great, meeting needs is not the foremost purpose. Seeing individuals come to Christ as Lord is the primary purpose. This does not mean that governmental affairs should be ignored. On the contrary, they must be addressed as the means by which the greater purpose of God's lordship is revealed.

Improve the situation of those who are underprivileged, neglected, hungry, homeless and victimized by prejudice, persecution and oppression (Matthew 22:39; Romans 13:8-10; 1 John 3:17). These passages emphasize the necessity of being sensitive to the needs of others. Compassion and mercy reveal the existence of true love (1 John 3:17), and Romans 13:8-10 stresses that loving others is the means by which the believer's obligations to the Lord are fulfilled.

The manner in which love and care is shown to those in need is the primary criterion. Matthew 25:35-40 describes the various needs: thirst, hunger, estrangement, imprisonment and need of clothing and protection. The parable of the Good Samaritan in Luke 10:30-37 emphasizes the need for sensitivity to the human needs of others. *Neighbor* comes from a Greek word meaning "near one." The Samaritan's ability to minister was based on moving near to the person in need and being a neighbor to him. In James 1:27, awareness of need was at the heart of what it means to be a devout child of God.

Protecting the Sanctity of Life

The third practice that reflects the discipleship value of social obligation is protecting the sanctity of life. Sanctity of life strikes a devout area of society. Christians are in a struggle to show the world that life is ultimately from God and rests in His hands. The following statement affirms the practice of recognizing the sanctity of life:

> *God alone confers life (Genesis 1:1-31); therefore, we are responsible to God to care for our physical life and that of others. If the circumstances require, we must be prepared to risk our life in the service of our neighbor (John 15:13); but the general rule is that we must respect our physical life and employ every worthy means to maintain it. Since God alone confers life, God alone must decide when it is to be ended (Psalm 31:14, 15). Because a human fetus is sacred and blessed of God, we believe we have the responsibility to protect the life of the unborn (Jeremiah 1:5; Luke 1:41). It is our firm conviction that abortion and euthanasia of the aged, mentally incompetent, terminally ill and otherwise handicapped, for reasons of personal convenience, social adjustment or economic advantage, are morally wrong.*

God alone confers life. The central message of the first chapter of the Bible is that God is the originator, designer and sustainer of life. He is the origin because the world was formed from His creative word, according to His good pleasure and will.

The sin of mankind is in not recognizing that God is sole originator, designer and sustainer of life. Mankind cannot create life. Such presumption becomes ineffective and destructive, falling short of God's will. Finally, man is not to determine the longevity or termination of life. To do so results in manipulation and murder. John 15:13 reflects God's command to honor and protect life.

God alone decides when life is to end (Psalm 31:14, 15). These verses emphasize a point made earlier in this section in connection with Genesis 1: God is the sustainer of life. Godliness places trust in the hand of God for the extension or termination of life.

Responsibility to protect the unborn (Jeremiah1:5; Luke 1:41). God has a relationship with the unborn that affirms their worth and valid existence as human beings. They are not merely biological tissues with no real connection with life after birth. In Jeremiah 1:5 the ministry of the prophet began in the womb of his mother. Jeremiah was already in relationship with God, fulfilling God's divine purposes before his birth. In Luke 1:41 the same was true of John the Baptist who, even before birth responded to the presence of the Holy Spirit.

Caring for the Earth and Its Resources

The fourth practice that reflects the discipleship value of social obligation is practicing care for the earth and its resources. This practice is affirmed in the following statement:

> *Furthermore, we believe it is our Christian responsibility to care for the earth and its resources. In the beginning God gave man dominion over the earth (Genesis 1:26-30). This does not, however, give us license to pollute our natural environment or to waste the resources of the earth.*

In Genesis 1:26-30, God gave the care of the earth into Adam's hands. The value of the earth is not rooted in its contents—it is based on its founder. The believer is to honor and responsively cultivate life on the earth as a child of God, not as a product of the earth. The heritage of the believer is the motivation to care for the earth, not the heritage as a member of the earth's society.

The believer's obligation to God concerning the earth is even more forceful when the overall context of these verses is considered. God commanded that the earth be cared for. Neglecting to do so is not just a waste of natural resources, it is a faith issue before anything else.

Additional Insights Into Social Obligation

Social obligation and stewardship. Christian service to others is not merely a social obligation, it is a responsibility the believer has to the Lord. Christ has entrusted the church with the ability and means to impact those in society at large. When believers love others in Christian service, they are being used as God's stewards in this world.

First Peter 4:10 expanded the concept of Christian love. God has given to all believers the ability to love and be hospitable to each other. It is a gift of ministry. The specific form of the gift may vary, but everyone has the ability to love one other.

The love for others described in 1 Peter is an act of stewardship. The concept of stewardship was built on the previous idea of a "gift." A steward managed and dispersed property and goods that belonged to someone else. In a similar way, love for those who are in need comes from God. God makes each believer a steward of that love.

The obligation to live in peace (Ephesians 4:26-32). The believer is obligated to live in peace with others. In this passage Paul speaks about various attributes that mark the believer's peace with God and others.

Peace with God (vv. 26-30). These verses review how anger, stealing and corrupt communication grieve the Holy Spirit.

Peace with others (vv. 31, 32). These verses describe ungodly, negative practices to avoid and positive, godly practices to maintain. Christians become a vessel of God's peace for others because peace with God has been established.

Paul listed attributes that the believer is able to contribute to society and the church. *Kindness* refers to actions that go beyond cordial gestures. The word in the Greek text stresses actions that are useful and beneficial for others. *Tenderhearted* refers to the compassion that should accompany these actions. *Forgiveness* is from a Greek word that actually means "to be obliging in relationship to others." It emphasizes having a favorable disposition toward others.

The walk of the believer in fulfilling social obligation. Social obligation can be accomplished by looking at the principles of the believers described by Paul in Ephesians 5.

God's children are followers (v. 1). Children are to follow their parents obediently and confidently. In similar fashion, the believer is to be a trusting and submissive follower of the Lord. *Followers* comes from the Greek word *mimatas*. The English word *mimic* is derived from this word and means to "imitate." This word in the New Testament is used primarily in the context of moral living.

God's children walk in love (v. 2). Paul called the Christian's manner of life a walk of love. *Walk* refers to someone's "conduct of life." Love is the boundary that defines that walk. The standard by which the believer's love is measured is Christ's own love. The word *as* sets the standard. Paul highlights Christ giving Himself "for us as an offering." This is an act of worship.

God's children forsake uncleanness (vv. 3, 4). Paul's teaching about forsaking uncleanness includes six prohibitions and one affirmation. The first three prohibitions highlight personal selfishness. The process of selfishness leads to fornication, uncleanness and covetousness. *Covetousness* means "to be greedy." All three refer to practices fulfilling personal lustfulness.

God's children do not partake with sinners (vv. 5-7). The people we associate with help to shape our lives. We become a reflection of them and they of us. This scripture admonishes believers to shun these sinful influences as much as possible.

Principles for overcoming injustice (Matthew 5:38-48). This is a section of the Sermon on the Mount delivered by Jesus. In the sermon Christ had already laid the foundation of His message by declaring the beatitudes (vv. 1-12). The theme of the message is that the righteousness of the Father might be fulfilled in the hearts of believers (vv. 17-20).

One of the areas of conduct that Jesus covered was injustice. The ability to overcome injustice is based on personal relationships with others, especially those who have done us wrong.

How we treat others who treat us unjustly, is a direct indication of our spiritual condition. Jesus taught in Matthew 5:39-42 that the believer should not retaliate to injustice, but provide for the needs of the individual. Retaliation seeks the demise of an individual. Provision responds to the person's well being.

The idea of retaliation was captured in the word *resist.* It comes from a word in the Greek text *anthisteemi,* which means "to set oneself against another." It calls for an action equal or greater in resistance to what was done. The problem is that resistance does not focus on restoration of the person.

Jesus responded by teaching that the needs and reconciliation of the other person, not elimination, should be the goal of the Christian. Non-violence is not the primary focus of Jesus' response. Verse 39 mentions the initial response of turning the other cheek. The focus of the believer's response is in verse 40, an extension and fulfillment of the response in verse 39. The final response of the believer is to give the "cloak" as an act of reconciliation, not just being non-violent.

The believer's response to injustice should not be passive, but provisional. In other words, when there is an injustice, the Christian should ask, "What need does this person have that I can meet?" This was Jesus' concern as He listed examples of this in verses 40-42.

Focusing on the needs of a wrongdoer does not mean that you aid in the injustice. This certainly was not the intention of Jesus' teaching. He did not say to perpetuate injustice. Rather, He taught that addressing the personal needs of the offender should be a significant part of the believer's response to injustice; meeting those needs are the ultimate response to injustice. Whereas the law in Leviticus 24:10-23 demanded retaliation and eventually death, Christ taught reconciliation and restoration.

Love your enemies (Matthew 5:43-48). In this section Jesus focused not only on those who do acts of injustice, but also on those who are actually our enemies. Some acts of injustice may be unintentional. Others may be occasional and not calculated. However, other acts are committed by those who have made themselves our enemies.

Jesus quoted from the Old Testament and referred to an interpretation of the Pharisees of His day. The quotation, "Thou shalt love thy neighbor," is from Leviticus 19:18. The interpretation, "Hate thine enemy," is from the interpretation of the Pharisees who had defined for themselves who one's neighbor was. They had scriptures such as the latter part of Deuteronomy 23:6, which discussed the enemies of God, and applied it to personal enemies.

Many qualified the quotation about loving their neighbor as someone who was friendly toward them. Therefore, they felt no obligation to love their enemy. The Old Testament law intended that enemies of God, such as the pagan nations described in Deuteronomy 23:6 who came against the nation of Israel, should be despised and rejected. The nations that tried to defeat Israel or draw her into backsliding were to be shunned, even destroyed.

The command to shun God's enemies as applied to personal enemies by the Pharisees is a flagrant violation of God's law. God has always sought love between individuals, even in the Old Testament. When an individual meets a stranger, or even a personal enemy, the individual's response is still to show love. An example of this was in Exodus 12:43-49 where the Israelites were to demonstrate love to those who traveled along with them, whether they were countrymen or not.

Response of Christ to enemies. Jesus gave a full response to the question of how to treat our enemies by outlining not one, but five different responses and profiles for loving our enemies.

The first item Jesus listed is the general call to "love your enemies." This is an amplification of the word *neighbor*, which included the person's enemies. *Enemy* comes from a Greek word that describes a person who "hates," "opposes" or is "hostile." The command to love extends even to that person.

The second item Jesus listed is to "bless them that curse you." *Curse* comes from a Greek word that means "to intend evil or doom upon someone." *Bless* means the opposite: to intend good or a blessing upon someone.

These words have spiritual as well as physical applications. The command means that even though the intentions or spiritual desires of an individual toward the believer are evil, the Christian is to pray for the spiritual well-being, with the best of intentions for that person.

The third item Jesus listed is to "do good to them that hate you." This item highlights the actions of love and the expected response someone might give to that love. Acts of love do not demand acts of love in return. On the contrary, Christians are to demonstrate love even when hatred is returned.

The fourth item taught by Jesus is to "pray for them that despitefully use you." This teaching includes times when there is little love that could be offered because the spite and hatred of the other individual. Acts of love may be nullified or prohibited by the hatred of another. They are able to dominate much of the love the Christian may show forth.

In this case the believer must continue in prayer. The temptation may be to become discouraged if it seems as though acts of love are ineffective. In the face of this kind of temptation, the love of the believer for an enemy can still be extended through the power of prayer.

The final teaching of Jesus addressed the category of persecution. He described the enemy as someone who may curse, hate or despitefully use the believer. Each of these descriptions becomes more intense and hateful. The final word, *persecute*, is the most aggressive. Even when the attitudes and actions of an enemy reach this degree, the believer must still respond with love, action and prayer.

Loving as a child of the Father (Matthew 5:45-48). After giving the commands to love our neighbor and enemy, Jesus used the example of the Father to emphasize the seriousness of the command.

When Jesus spoke of the Father's love, He referred to His unbiased concern for all, even the evil and unjust. God's love does not stop at the doorway of evil. It continues into the heart and life of those who are His enemies. There will be an ultimate day of judgment for the unjust. However, first the light of God's love will be cast on them.

The extent of God's love as described by Jesus is far reaching. Jesus used Old Testament references of God's sun and rain, His blessings and provisions being extended to the evil and unjust, as well as the good and the just. There is no measuring or dividing considered. The love of God reaches out to everyone—regardless of the condition of the individual's heart.

Jesus did not explain how or why the Father loved in that way—He only compared His love to the prejudice of the publicans. The Father's love is justly given, with no qualifying or discriminating factors. The actions of the publicans, on the other hand, were based on status and wealth. The publicans were the tax collectors of that day. They took too much from the impoverished and gave preferential treatment to the economic and political elite. Their kindness was based on the benefits they would receive in return. By comparison, the love of the Father is extended to everyone, even those who work against Him. Christian love is not just a matter of principle. It is a demonstration of membership in the family of God

Social obligation and overcoming evil with godliness (Romans 12:14-21). Paul emphasized the teaching of Jesus from the Sermon on the Mount by writing about loving one's enemies in Romans 12. In these verses Paul dealt with the proper reaction of the Christian to four different situations. Each is under the same heading of Jesus' teaching about loving our enemies and not responding to the unjust.

1. *Persecution.* The believer's ministry when being persecuted is to "bless and curse not." To *bless* means to beseech God for His mercy and blessings to rest upon that person. This response does not condone the actions of the person. The response is to convict and ultimately draw the person to fuller blessings of God.

2. *Rejoicing over sin is never appropriate.* Jesus' teaching addressed the temptation to despise the rejoicing of someone considered an enemy. Jesus' command does not refer to acts of sin. It applies to personal rejoicing in joyful situations. On those occasions, the believer is to rejoice for the fortune of the other person.

The principle of rejoicing applies to weeping as well. When even an enemy has a time of personal weeping and grief, the believer should not succumb to the temptation to gloat or rejoice. Rather, the burden should be shared and the hope of eventual reconciliation kept alive. These times of grief can be an opportunity to display the compassion of the Lord.

3. *Preferential treatment.* The final situation Jesus described is the issue of preferential attitudes and treatment. Believers should never feel that they are any better than anyone else. The call of this passage is to be "of the same mind." In Romans 12 Paul applies the believer's personal sacrifice of service to the Lord (vv. 1, 2) to everyday life. We are to hold things in mutual love and respect, reaching even the impoverished and destitute. No economic, social or political bias is to be shown.

The exhortation in verse 16, "Be not wise in your own conceits," is the primary motivation for division and preferential love. A person, based upon self-centered perceptions, can begin to feel they are better than others. That feeling leads to insensitivity toward others. Whatever acts of love are then shown, are shown only according to limited and selfish perceptions.

Living peaceably. In verses 17 and 18, Paul defines peace based on honesty rather than recompense. The word *recompense* refers to love given on the basis of returning to others what has been done to you.

In the case of the word *honesty*, Paul is appealing to the principles discussed throughout Romans 12—love as a service to God. Honest love, based on the love and care of the Lord, is the basis of true and lasting peace. The actions of an individual should not guide the Christian's response. If that were the case, the responses would indeed be evil for evil. However, love always endures and becomes a lasting testimony and witness of the power of God.

The key to demonstrating this kind of love is found in the phrase "as much as lieth in you." God's provision to love is never lacking. The only deficiency occurs when we fail to allow God to work in us and when we focus our love on the actions of others.

Overcoming evil with good (vv. 19, 21). The foundation and motivation for loving others runs parallel to other concerns. The first issue is whether injustices will ever be made right. The second issue is to what extent are good works effective in the face of evil.

There is a temptation to distort these issues and think that we must make things right, thereby forgetting the work of God. Many times waiting on God's justice can be frustrating and agonizingly long. The temptation is to think good works are wasted and ineffective when given to the unlovable and the unjust.

Verses 19-21 dispute these temptations. God will always make injustices right. Man-made justice is only temporary. Evil never corrects evil, but God provides the grace for overcoming evil.

Christian witness is a matter of living out our faith in a godly and loving manner that follows the example of Christ as He responded to His enemies.

Church of God Historical Review

The earliest records of the General Assembly note occasional references to issues of social obligation. There were a number of statements made in the 1908 General Assembly and a few in subsequent Assemblies. However, after the outbreak of World War II, the church became more involved with social action. There was another lull in social involvement until the advent of resolutions in the 1950's. They became a major way in which the church addressed social issues. Also, while the church did not formulate official statements or decisions regarding race, the involvement of black ministers and congregations in the assembly can be noted in the Minutes.

The Church of God has had long-standing commitment to the family and the rights of infants, especially the unborn. One of the strongest statements regarding the unborn was from a resolution adopted in 1974.

ABORTION....WHEREAS life originated in the creative work of Almighty God, and ...WHEREAS man himself is created in the image and likeness of God, and ...WHEREAS God assigned special value to human life, and ...WHEREAS Divine law forbids the indiscriminate taking of human life, exacting heavy penalites of those who violate this commandment, and...

WHEREAS contemporary society demonstrates a low esteem for the sacredness of life, and...WHEREAS abortion on demand now receives serious consideration as a means of birth and population control, and ...WHEREAS abortion is a vicious attack on the weakest and most help-less form of human life, and ...WHEREAS the unborn are unable to speak in their own defense, and...WHERE-AS intense pressure is being brought upon state and national legislative bodies to liberalize abortion laws, and ...WHEREAS it is the duty of the Church to raise an authoritative moral voice concerning this vital issue ...BE IT RESOLVED That we, the General Assembly of the Church of God, reaffirm our historic commitment to the sacredness of human life, and...BE IT FURTHER RESOLVED That we stand opposed to the use of abor-tion as a means of birth or population control, and ...BE IT FURTHER RESOLVED That we urge our entire con-stituency to actively oppose any liberalization of abortion laws by state legislatures and by the Congress of the United States, and ...BE IT FURTHER RESOLVED That no individual should ever consider abortion as an option except in the gravest circumstances, after medical and religious consultation of the most serious nature (*Minutes,* 1974, pp. 35-6).

The third Assembly in 1908 dealt with several issues relating to the church and its relationship to the govern-ment. The discussions also included relationships with lodges. The record read as follows:

At 11-15 M.S. Lemons in an address impressed upon the assembly the importance of the themes and subjects for discussion....Noon....1 P.M. Prayer service by W.F. Bryant....1-30 Diverged from order of program on ac-count of the absence of one on duty and 'Sundry sub-jects'were discussed. Viz. Our duty about voting. Can church members belong to lodges? Worshiping God as conscience may dictate. The uniting of Church and state, The law and its relations to the Church. R.G. Spurling opened the subjects followed by H.L. Trim, Alex Hamby, W.F. Bryant and J.H. Simpson. The following was the final conclusion on all these subjects by the assembly. Viz. 1. Church members should vote provided they can do so with a clear conscience. 2. No person that belongs to a lodge is eligible to membership of the Lords Church. 2 Cor. 6:14-17. Eph. 5:4-7,11,12. 2 Tim. 3:4,5. and Math 5:34-37., Jas. 5:12. and expositions as to the laws and practices were given as a reason for the above decision. 3. Should obey laws so long as said laws do not conflict with Christ's law, 4. Would be mockery to worship God contrary to a mans conscience but his conscience should be purged, and trained according to the laws and commands of Jesus. 5. Opposed to the union of Church and state under any circumstances. 6. The church should appreciate the laws that protect public worship and should recognize the officers of the law as God's ministers. Romans 13:1-6.

A notation on lodges was the only item to appear in the business of the Assembly for several years. The committee also drafted the original Church of God Teachings that were approved by the Assembly. The question about lodges gave insight into the primary concern of the Assembly. That concern was that they were "secret" and called for allegiance that rivaled allegiance to Christ. The question was first listed in the 1910 church paper along with the Teachings, "Are you free from any connection whatever with lodges or secret orders?" (1910 *The Evening Light and Church of God Evangel*, August 15, 1910, Vol. 1, No. 12, p. 3).

In the January, 1913 General Assembly the topics of lodges, secret orders and a specific union was discussed. The notation was as follows, "Can any one belonging to a lodge or secret order be received into the Church of

God? This question has been amply dealt with in the past and the answer is emphatically, No!"

The item on lodges was also added to the list of teachings of the church in 1914. It read, "Against members belonging to lodges—John 18:20, 2 Corinthians 6:14-17" (*1914 General Assembly Minutes,* p. 47). The General Overseer addressed the topic in a speech in the 1917 General Assembly when he said, "We do not want any that are members of lodges or secret orders. They must lay down all such orders before they come into the

A similar item was listed in the 1925 *General Assembly Minutes* regarding the Klu Klux Klan and oath-bound societies. The item was printed in 1925 as part of the Supplement to the Minutes from 1931 to 1936. The record was as follows:

> "Shall a member of the Church of God be permitted to belong to the K.K.K., or shall he be permitted to join the Klan after he is a member of the Church of God? The Assembly has already passed that our members shall not belong to any oath bound- society (*1925 General Assembly Minutes*, p. 40).

There was a notation regarding labor unions in the January, 1913 General Assembly. The 1915 Assembly dealt further with the issue, making certain decisions. These decisions were later amended in the 1917, and 1928. The four items were as follows:

> Q. Can any one belonging to the united Coal Miners' Association be received into the Church of God? A. The question might cover labor unions of all kinds. This matter has been looked into and studied carefully from every viewpoint. The time will come when we cannot buy nor sell unless we have the mark of the beast in hand or forehead. It is a matter of bread and butter, but we do

not dare to compromise and be bound by an order to bestow a favor upon a member of such order in preference to a brother of the household of faith. The question has been answered before with a positive, No!" (January, 1913 *General Assembly*, pp. 67-8)

Attention was called to the membership and labor union question and concluding minute read. At the close of the reading the entire congregation was melted under the mighty hand of God as He so wonderfully set His seal of approval upon it. On account of it being so vividly demonstrated that the Lord was pleased with it, it was unanimously accepted and it could have been truthfully said, It seemed good to the Holy Ghost and us. After the decision was made by the Holy Ghost the whole assembly kneeled before God and wept and gave thanks to His name. The decision as read: The Assembly of the Churches of God stand for the full standard laid down in the Bible. Therefore, the members of the Church of God shall not be members of any lodge or labor union, nor voluntarily pay any dues to them for any cause. If, however, the company by which members are employed holds back a part of their wages for any cause such members are not responsible, but it is happened unto them according to the Scriptures 'Behold, the hire of the laborers who have reaped down your fields,...is... kept back by fraud" (1915 *General Assembly Minutes*, p. 19).

[From address by General Overseer]"The matter of labor unions seems more difficult, but we do not want any that voluntarily belong to labor unions and attend their meetings and willingly pay their dues. But should the employers hold back their dues, and if dues are takes as a tax, or to buy the privilege of working, it is considered in harmony with the Scripture that shows the hire of the laborers to be kept back by fraud (See 1915 minutes)" (1917 General Assembly Minutes, p. 28).

That the restriction concerning labor unions be lifted where it is strictly necessary to belong to them in order to obtain or retain employment. However, we want it understood that the Church of God does not endorse labor unions" (1928 General Assembly, p. 25)

A few statements were made in the 1917 General Assembly regarding life in the community and relating to governmental authorities. The statements were as follows:

Q. Can we be compelled by the laws to hold up our hand and swear in court? Ans. No. The law provides that we can affirm without holding up our hand. Q. Should our members be courteous to those in authority? Ans. Yes, due courtesy must be shown to officers and all in authority, and says, honor them to whom honor is due. Q. Shall members of the church be jurymen in court? Ans. Members are advised to keep out of the jury as much as possible, and if you are compelled to act, use your very best judgment in the case according to law and evidence. Those who do not believe in capital punishment are not allowed to sit on a jury in a murder case. . . . Advices to Members . . . Show your love and fellowship to every one without partiality. . . . Show special courtesy to strangers who may chance to fall in with you in your meetings. . . . Always live a good straight life at home and abroad so no one can justly think or speak of you as a hypocrite. Guard your conversation. Be careful what you say about a brother, sister or anyone. . . . Younger members should not company or associate too intimately with worldly outsiders. Members should never marry sinners..." (*1917 General Assembly Minutes*, p. 48).

There was very little mentioned in the General Assembly Minutes regarding World War I. The only record of comment or business before, during or after the war was an addition to the list of teachings in 1917. The original teaching is given below along with subsequent decisions and revisions:

29. Against members going to war—Exodus 20:13, 1 Chronicles 28:3, Psalm 120.7, Luke 22.49-52, John 18.10,11,36. Romans 12.19" *1917 General Assembly Minutes*, p. 65).

In 1921 Article 29 on war was omitted. [In 1928 Article 29 reinstated with "...in combatant service" added.] In 1945 Article 29 replaced with the following:

The Church of God believes that nations can and should settle their differences without going to war; however, in the event of war, if a member engages in combatant service, it will not affect his status with the Church. In case a member is called into military service who has conscientious objections to combatant service, the Church will support him in his constitutional rights (1945 General Assembly, p. 31).

CHAPTER TWELVE

FORMING DISCIPLESHIP VALUES IN THE CHURCH

D iscipleship values are not a private matter. Scripture is the source of the believer's values. Interpreting Scripture and forming values comes from the believer working with the body of Christ. Even in the early church, warnings were given against privately interpreting the Scripture because truth was corrupted by isolationism. Peter warned the church against the fallacy of developing interpretations and morality separate from other believers.

> Knowing this first, that no prophecy of the scripture is of any private interpretion. For the prophecy came not in old time by the will of man: but holy men of God spake as they were moved by the Holy Ghost. But there were false prophets also among the people, even as there shall be false teachers among you, who privily shall bring in damnable heresies even denying the Lord that bought them, and bring upon themselves swift destruction. And many shall follow their pernicious ways; by reason of whom the way of truth shall be evil spoken of (2 Peter 1:20—2:2).

The process of forming discipleship values must be developed within the context of the church. Part of the context of the church includes the manner in which it has solved difficult moral problems. In the development of faith and practice critical questions arise. The way the church solves its problems of faith and living can serve as an example for individual believers.

The church must discern the will of God for the body. The church cannot proceed with goals centered around God unless it can perceive what God is doing in the world. This is a strong claim . . . to know what God is doing in the world. However, if the church does not seek this end, it will be just another organization doing good deeds.

Faithfulness to the values of God is the first priority of the church. Identification of these values is important. However, values must always be confessed as the goals that God desires.

Each believer participates in the discernment and desire for the presence and power of God in everyday living. The study of the Word, the teaching ministries, the worship in song and praise, and the ministries of the church should enhance the believer's search for the power and presence of the Lord.

Individual Believers and the Church Form Discipleship Values Together

The task of establishing the priority of God's will begins in the life of each believer and extends to participation within the body of Christ. The believer must foster skills of personal discipleship. The ministries of the church should equip the laity to study the Word and call individuals to a life of prayer. Each person should be taught the priority of family relationships as an extension of Christian discipleship (Ephesians 5:21—6:4; Colossians 3:18-21). These areas are the means by which individual believers discern the will of God.

Love within the community of the church must be fostered by the organization of the church. In other words, the church should organize administrative functions and activities that encourage love for each other. The structure of the church should invite communion with God and other believers. Recognition of the ministry of each person in the Body fosters this kind of love. Love for other believers is part of the salvation message of the church (John 13:34, 35). These are ways the church can affirm God's will for love to abide in the church.

The ministry of the church to the world is an outgrowth of God working through individuals and believers loving one another. This can be diagramed as follows:

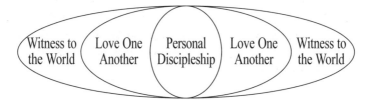

Personal discipleship results in love for one another. Love for one another results in a witness to the world. If there is no personal discipleship, love for one another will be diminished. If love for one another is diminished, then the church's witness to the world will be ineffective.

This process does not negate the recording of the history and testimony of a church's tradition and practice. In fact, it is necessary. Without the preserved testimonies of the people of God, succeeding generations will lose strength and wisdom.

Paul appealed to the Colossians to use the traditions they had in a Christ-centered way. Tradition, history, and remembrance in and of itself is not wrong. It is the focus given to these that creates confusion in the church. The focus of the traditions and memory retained by a church must center around Christ. This is what Paul meant in Colossians 2:8 when he said they must not be "of men" but "after Christ."

This history is part of the continuing witness of the church to the world.

- It provides power and insight to future generations.

- It carries on the work and influence of previous generations.

- It keeps the church from merely seeking short-term, temporary goals.

Such short sightedness focuses on the finite, immediate concerns of men rather than on the abiding, infinite testimonies of the Lord. Maintaining the history of a body of believers, centered around God, encourages fellowship and seeks the continuing power and presence of the Lord.

Develop Discipleship Values

The equipping of the believer is a reminder that God is active in individual lives. God empowers believers and gives them gifts to carry out His will through the life of the church. Organization in the church helps facilitate this equipping and formation process.

Clear guidelines and doctrinal statements enhance the believer's perception of God's values for living. These statements communicate the church's intention and commitment to the will and work of God.

The Role of Being a Spiritual Example

Matthew 6 is quoted a number of times in the first section of the Practical Commitments to make this point. Verse 5 admonishes the believer not to be hypocritical. The word, *hypocrite*, comes from a Greek word, *hupocritos,* which means, "to wear a mask." This reference was actually warning against insincere displays of worship before others. A premium must be placed on personal devotions as the foundation for being a spiritual example.

The Role of Moral Purity as a Sacrifice Unto God

Moral purity is emphasized in Scripture through many concepts including Romans 12:1, 2. These verses encourage us to present ourselves as a living sacrifice to God. The way that we monitor our lifestyles is a service of worship to God. Moral purity is not intended to preserve a man-made lifestyle or code of ethics. Rather, it should follow a discipline of living that can be an instrument of worship to God.

The Example of the Early Church

Acts 15 and 16 provide a picture of the church solving difficult problems and developing values for the believer. The principles from this text apply to the believer today. This chapter will discuss some important principles for the development of faith and practice.

A study of Acts 15 indicates the following process is a Biblical pattern for the Pentecostal church today:

- Calling a group of representatives together

- Discussing vital issues of personal morality

- Being led by leaders such as James in the decision process

- Arriving at a consensus regarding personal morality issues and

- Issuing the decision for circulation with the expectation that it be followed.

All of these elements are in the process described in Acts 15 and 16. It was not an easy process, but the results were growth in faith and practice for believers. The same is true today.

The Holy Spirit Turns Morality Into Discipleship

The disciples were faced with a dilemma. Jesus had just announced His departure. It was bad enough that their treasurer had just left, but now the Lord himself had just said He was departing. That same evening, the Lord had led them in supper, speaking of things about His body and blood they did not fully understand. He then washed their feet—a highly uncustomary practice. Their leader, the One who had changed their lives, the One that some of them felt they could die for, was now doing unusual things. One of their own was betraying the Master. And, on top of everything, He announced that He was leaving.

The description of this setting is in John 13. The disciples were at their lowest point. The life that they were living and their hopes for their futures had faded with the Lord's announced departure. The disciples were exactly that, "disciples." They were followers of Jesus. They had forsaken all for Him (Matthew 19:27). They had been changed from fishermen, a tax collector, a physician and many other walks of life to become His disciples. Now He was leaving. Or was He?

As the disciples began asking questions of Jesus in John 13—16, the Lord explained that He was going to be with the heavenly Father, but their discipleship and formation process would not stop. The principles would be the same. He would still be the key to their becoming disciples. They would learn from Him, even though He would not be physically present.

The heart of Jesus' explanation was the Holy Spirit. The Holy Spirit would bring Jesus' presence to them to walk with them as He had walked with them before. Jesus' words to them were:

> Jesus answered and said unto him, If a man love me, he will keep my words: and my Father will love him, and we will come unto him, and make our abode with him. He that loveth me not keepeth not my sayings: and the works which ye hear is not mine, but the Father's which sent me. These things have I spoken unto you, being yet present with you. But the Comforter, which is the Holy Ghost, whom the Father will send in my name, he shall teach you all things, and bring all things to your remembrance, whatsoever I have said unto you (John 14:23-26).

Jesus desired that they have peace. He expected them to follow His commandments. Love for God and one another is essential to discipleship. Learning about the things Christ taught them is very important. Start HereBeing a witness in the world would result from all that would happen to them. All of these elements would depend upon the work of the Holy Spirit in their lives.

Jesus covered many subjects as He taught His disciples in John 13-17, but one issue He emphasized was that He would be with them through the ministry and presence of the Holy Spirit. Though He was going away, the Comforter (the Holy Spirit) would be with them, and the

Lord would also be "in them" (17:26) through the Holy Spirit.

The new reality of Christ's presence would impact their lives more than before. Christ would no longer be observable but He would be abiding within them. He would no longer be heard through their ears but He would penetrate their very thoughts. He would no longer be felt externally but He would be felt deep within them. Their growth as disciples would be on a much deeper level because of the work of Christ through the Holy Spirit.

Christ's desire was that they abide in Him (15:7). They were to be so close to them that they would actually be connected to Him, just as a vine branch was connected to the main vine (vv. 1-8). They would develop even more than they had thus far. Just as a vine grows, they would grow and even bear fruit (v. 8). This new process of growing as disciples and then reproducing disciples for the Lord would be accomplished through the presence and work of the Holy Spirit.

The Holy Spirit and Peace for the Disciples

Jesus knew the disciples were troubled. He was very concerned as well. He was launching them into a new dimension as disciples. They would no longer walk physically with Him but they would walk in the Spirit. They had to be assured in their hearts about the trans-mission. Furthermore, the Lord desired that they prosper in their hearts and experience joy, peace and love. Finally he not only wanted them to have these experiences but He also wanted them to receive them in full measure.

Right after telling them that they would have the Comforter, the Holy Spirit, He said they would have peace (14:27). At the same time, the Lord said they would have love and joy (v. 28). Throughout His teaching, Jesus spoke of the many experiences they would have because of His work and presence through the Holy Spirit. Their joy would remain (15:11). Their peace would continue in even the worse circumstances (16:33). Their joy would be His joy fulfilled in them (17:13). Paul later testified to the truth of Christ's teaching when he reminded the disciples that the fruit of the Spirit was love, joy, peace, longsuffering, gentleness, goodness, faith, meekness and temperance (Galatians 5:22, 23); all the experiences that Jesus said would happen.

The Holy Spirit and the Commandments of the Lord

The Holy Spirit would aid the disciples in keeping the commandments of the Lord, a strong desire of the Lord. The Lord reminded the disciples how important it was for them to obey His commandments. Keeping the commandments was a demonstration of the disciple's love for God and a key to the love of the Father abiding in them. Keeping His commandments was important for the presence of the God to abide in them (14:23, 24). Keeping His commandments was important for the joy of the Lord to abide in them (15:11). Christ indicated that He was emphasizing His commandments while being with the disciples, but once He would physically leave them, the Holy Spirit would fulfill the role of emphasizing the commandments (14:25, 26).

The Holy Spirit and Learning From the Lord

The name given the Holy Spirit by the Lord in John 14:26 was *Comforter,* a name which meant teacher and trainer. The disciples were not only to keep the commandments of the Lord, but they were also *disciples,* a word which is synonymous with our contemporary word *student*. The Holy Spirit would be their teacher and trainer. Being a trainer meant that the transmission of knowledge was only the first step. Their behavior would be changed. Their motivation would be changed. Their values would be changed. They would be trained in the commandments of the Lord by the Comforter.

Christ described the work of the Comforter:

- To "teach" them (14:26).

- To help them "bear much fruit" as disciples (15:8).

- To "testify" of the Christ and the truth of Christ (15:27).

- To "guide" them into all truth (16:13).

- To show them things to come (16:13).

- To "glorify" Christ (16:14).

Love was the key ingredient to the formation of the disciples and the Holy Spirit's work in them. When Christ first announced to the disciples that He was departing, He gave them the "new commandment" of love (13:33, 34). The commandment that they love one another was so decisive, it would be the key to others being able to identify them as disciples of the Lord (13:35). The love that they would have would not be mere human love, but it would be the same love that the heavenly Father had loved Him with. This extraordinary love would now be exchanged between them through the enablement of the Holy Spirit (14:25, 26).

The Holy Spirit and Being a Witness of the Lord

Christ taught that a disciple would be a living witness to the world. A true disciple is at the same time a witness.

A disciple does not witness once and a while. The fact that a person is a disciple is a testimony to the world.

The world would be against the disciples not because of anything they did, but because of Christ. The world crucified Christ. Christ would be abiding in them through the Holy Spirit. The world would still come after Christ. Before it was the physical presence of Christ. Now, they would come after the presence of Christ within the disciples.

The Holy Spirit's role would be multi-faceted in the witness of the disciples:

- To bring the abiding presence of the Lord to the disciple (14:26).

- To instruct the disciples in the love of the Lord that would be further witness to the world that they were His disciples (13:34-35).

- To encourage the disciples when they would be confronted by the world because of their witness 14:27-28).

- To keep the disciples in the way of truth so they would not be manipulated by the challenges of the world (15:26).

The woes and challenges by the world would be many for the disciples. They would have trouble (15:18-25). They would be judged by the world (16:1-11). They would have sorrow because of the world (16:20-28). Essentially, the disciples would not be of the world (17:14-16). However, because of the provision of the Holy Spirit, the disciples would be able to experience the overcoming victory of the Lord (16:31-33).

Summary

Discipleship values are more than abstract philosophies—they are works of the Holy Spirit in the believer. These values are more than the words and teachings of Jesus—they are His words and works manifest in and through His disciples. The values of the Christian are not just works. They are the deeds of the risen Christ through His church.

The Holy Spirit is the transformer that moves the disciple beyond words into a new reality. The ethic of the disciple's value system is not just something for everyday living, it is an eternal witness of the living Lord. The Holy Spirit is the teacher of values for the disciple. The Holy Spirit transforms believers from mere moral persons to disciples of the living Lord.